YOUR ~~GUIDE~~ S0-AAA-830

To The Irish Pubs Of Boston

4th EDITION

Publisher
Green Line Publishing, Inc.
PO Box 813
Medford, MA 02155
greenlinepub@gmail.com

Compiled and Edited by
Charles Kelley and Jim Molis

Sponsored by
Diageo-Guinness USA

Index

SPECIAL ADVERTISING SECTION AFTER PAGE 72

THE MAN BEHIND THE LEGACY - ARTHUR GUINNESS

The Guinness Family

Arthur founded a dynasty that controlled the Brewery for 227 years. He himself did his bit for posterity by fathering 21 children, although only 10 survived. His descendants showed themselves to be equally prolific, ensuring a steady supply of candidates for the top job, all of whom shared his philanthropy, energy and longevity.

From $150 to Global Empire

When the Archbishop of Cashel drew up his will, he could not have imagined that one day his godson would use his legacy of £100 to found one of the greatest brewing empires in the world. Arthur inherited the money at the age of 27 and honed his skills with a small brewery in Leixlip in County Kildare. Four years later he set off for the bright lights of Dublin...

9000 Year Lease

That Arthur was a shrewd and canny entrepreneur has never been in question. Yet some might say signing a 9,000 year lease on a run down brewery was pushing it a bit. Arthur signed the lease for approx. $60.00 per year!

Energy and Self Belief

Success did not come easily. Arthur fought every step of the way to build his empire, and above all to secure that most essential of natural resources, water. Arthur did not lack energy or self-belief so although that particular fight took him 12 years to win, win it he did. At the time Arthur set up in Dublin, there were 200 breweries in Ireland, and 10 just in St. James's Street alone. And they were all there for one simple reason - access to a pure and guaranteed water supply. It's no surprise then that when the City Sheriff's team turned up one day in 1775 to cut off Arthur's supply, his usual reserve deserted him. He grabbed a pickaxe from one of the men and announced himself prepared to "defend it by force of arms." Less dramatically perhaps, it was force of law and perseverance that finally won the battle for Arthur.

Origins of the Black Stuff

Arthur Guinness originally brewed ale which had to be served from a blend of several barrels. He noted that a popular "Black Beer" was being exported by London Brewers to Dublin. This beer was popular with the porters of Covent Garden and was known as "Entire" in that it was served from a single barrel. Seeing a great opportunity, Arthur tried his hand at brewing this new beer, and had more success than his fellow Dublin brewers. He chose this new beer above his ales and Guinness was born. In 1799, when Arthur was 74, he brewed his last ale.

Fun Guinness Facts

· A pint of Guinness cost about 1¢ in 1900.
· Doctors once prescribed Guinness as a cure for debility, anemia and to help patients through their convalescence.
· In Dublin in the 1800's, ale was drunk instead of poorly sanitized water.
· By 1930, a total of 13,940 people (excluding wives, families or other dependents) relied on the brewery for their income.
· The water for the St James's Gate Brewery in Dublin is fed by the waters from St James's Well in County Kildare.
· Guinness used to be recommended to nursing mothers.
· The lease was originally a rent of £45 per year and the deal included a copper, a kieve, a mill, two malt houses, stables for 12 horses and a loft for 200 tons of hay ... Bargain !!!

A Guinness Timeline

1752 ... .Arthur inherits $150 from his uncle and sets up a small brewery in Leixlip, County Kildare.
1759 ... .Arthur leases St. James Gate brewery for £100 down, and signs a lease for £45 per year for 9000 years.
1794 ... .First record of Guinness being drunk in London.
1799 ... .Arthur stopped brewing ale.
1802 ... .West Indies porter was exported to the West Indies.
1821 ... .Guinness Extra Stout porter first brewed.
1862 ... .Guinness label introduced featuring the Harp device.
1913 ... .A shipment of Guinness sinks with the Titanic.
1935 ... .Toucan first used in advertising.
1955 ... .First Guinness Ad on TV.
1959 ... .Draught Guinness launched in the UK.
1961 ... .Draught Guinness launched in Ireland.
1967 ... .Draught Guinness introduced into the USA.
1989 ... .Draught Guinness in cans launched in Great Britain

SIX STEPS TO POURING THE PERFECT PINT OF GUINNESS

Pouring and serving the perfect Guinness® pint is part science and part art. We were schooled on the subject by Guinness brewmaster Fergal Murray. Here's what we learned:

Guinness Brewmaster
Fergal Murray

"Six Degrees of Preparation"
Guinness Draught is best served at 6°C (that's 42.8°F), with the legendary two-part, six-step, pour. The steps are demonstrated by the lovely Nicole Szuminski of Flann O'Brien's in Mission Hill; in our opinion Boston's supreme pint-pourer.

1. The Glass: Start with a clean, dry, tulip-shaped pint glass...and that'll be a 20 ounce "Imperial" pint; not the "junior" 16 ounce variety.

2. The Angle: Hold the glass at a 45° angle and never allow the spout to touch the glass, or the beer in the glass.

3. The Pour: Pull the faucet down and allow the beer to fill the glass. You will see the surge commence. Allow the beer to flow smoothly into the angled glass and fill it three-quarters of the way.

The Angle and The Pour

4. The Head: Set the glass down and allow the beer to settle. You'll see the bubbles actually flowing downward along the sides of the glass. The glass is aerodynamically designed so the bubbles flow back up the middle and help create the creamy head.

5. The Top-Up: After the beer has settled (there will be a distinct gap between the dark liquid and the head) the glass is topped up slowly to create a domed effect with the head looking proudly over the glass.

The Top-Up

The Presentation

6. The Presentation: Present your Perfect Pint to an adoring customer.

It takes 119.5 seconds to pour the perfect pint. But don't fret. It's worth the wait.

SMITHWICK'S ALE

Smithwick's® (pronounced "Smit-ticks") Irish Ale is an ale with a clean, refreshing taste that balances bittering hops and roasted barley for a flavor that mixes a slightly sweet malt with moderate bitterness; all natural according to the goodness of Guinness.

Saint Francis Abbey Brewery in Kilkenny is situated on the site of a Franciscan abbey where monks had brewed ale since the 14th century, and has ruins of the original abbey on its grounds. It is Ireland's oldest operating brewery, founded by John Smithwick in 1710 on land owned by the Duke of Ormonde. Each day the brewery produces 8,000 kegs of Smithwick's Ale that are enjoyed the world over.

The first export of Smithwick's Irish Ale to the United States was shipped to Boston in January 1950. Guinness & Co. started exporting Smithwick's Irish Ale to the United States in 2004. All Smithwick's sold in the United States is brewed in Ireland. In the Monde Selection Beer Tasting Competition, Smithwick's earned five gold medals.

HARP LAGER

Harp Lager was born in 1959 when the Great Northern Brewery, which had been established in Dundalk, County Louth, as an ale and stout brewery in 1897, was acquired by Harp Lager Brewery Ltd. The name and the Brian Boru Harp emblem pay tribute to the Guinness logo and the national symbol of Ireland. It was early 1960 that brewing got under way, and by June 1960 the first bottle appeared on sale in Ireland.

Brewed in Canada, Harp has a sparkling, golden color with a crisp clean flavor enriched by its pleasing aroma. Unlike other beers that use rice and corn fillers, Harp Lager contains only malted barley. Harp contains Saaz & Hallertau hops from Germany & The Czech Republic and uses lager yeast from Bavaria.

Introduction

Welcome to the fourth edition of YOURGUIDE™ To The Irish Pubs Of Boston, your passport to 242 of the best Irish pubs in and around our great city.

In previous editions we've spoken of the great renaissance of the Irish pub occurring in Boston over the past dozen years or so. Well, it continues. Wonderful new Irish pubs continue to pop up in and around the city. Pubs of such quality that they quickly earn their place alongside the old, familiar favorites. These new pubs were one reason we decided to update the guide. Another reason was that we wanted to spread our wings a bit further; including the Worcester area, in a guide that also reaches up into southern New Hampshire and down to Cape Cod & The Islands. We feel we've put together the most comprehensive guide possible for local Irish pub afficionados. We're sure you'll find your perfect pub, your personal patch of Irish heaven, right here in this book.

There's one more reason we decided it was time to update the guide: we simply love what we do. As much as all these wonderful pubs have filled us with fond memories, perhaps our fondest are of the people we've met along the way. We'd like to thank Eilish at the Somers Pubs Group, Michael from The Druid, Stu from Honey Fitz, Shane from Hugh O'Neill's, Artie from Kitty O'Shea's, Declan from Lir, Sean at McFadden's, Mary at The Elephant & Castle, Brendan at Tommy Moloney's, Jill at The Briar Group, Sean at Porterbelly's and David at The Pub Sign Shop. We couldn't possibly name all the kind people who provided us with a jolt of the craic when we needed it; but to you all: Cheers!

Special appreciation goes out to the book's sponsor, the good folks at Diageo-Guinness USA, particularly the terrific group we worked with on this project; Aidan Fallon and Becky MacGregor. We're all aware of the deep respect for the culture of Irish pubs and unwavering commitment to quality that is found throughout the Guinness brands. We can tell you from firsthand experience that the same is true of their people and we raise a pint of the good stuff to each of them.

Charles Kelley
Jim Molis
Green Line Publishing, Inc.

DOWNTOWN, FANEUIL HALL, NORTH STATION

An Tain

31 India Street   617.426.1870

open Mon - Fri 11am 'til 2am
Sat 6pm 'til 2am, Closed Sun

The restaurant at An Tain is a unique dining experience for discriminating tastes. The bar is perfect for an after work release and has a high-energy atmosphere at night.

Food: Kitchen is open 11am 'til 9pm Monday through Friday. The cuisine is Creative American and includes a selection of soups, sandwiches, roll-ups, salads and appetizers complimented by a few entrees. A couple favorites are the Baked Haddock and Steak Tips. Daily specials.

Entertainment: A DJ entertains Friday and Saturday 10pm - 2am.

What's In A Name: An Táin Bó Cúailnge is the oldest written legend in Ireland. The tale relates a war against Ulster by the Connacht queen Medb and her husband Ailill, who intend to steal the stud bull Donn Cuailnge, and the efforts of the teenage Ulster hero Cúchulainn to oppose them.

Biddy Early's

141 Pearl Street   617.654.9944

open Mon - Sat 10:30am 'til 2am,
closed Sun

Located in the heart of the financial district, Biddy Early's is decorated in historic decor with knicknacks from Eire. It's typical of the pubs of Ireland from long ago. Very popular with the business lunch crowd.

Food: Served daily 11am 'til 11pm. Popular offerings are the marinated Steak Tips, juicy 8oz. burgers, Beef Stew, Shepherd's Pie with Creamy Mash, Fish & Chips and Stacked Nachos like you've never had before - with chili, cheese, olives, jalapeños, salsa and sour cream. Always a few specials.

Entertainment: Dart boards and TVs. There are occasional live music performances.

What's In A Name: Biddy Early was a witch from County Clare, born in 1798. She was said to be a great hand at helping folks, by looking into her blue bottle like a crystal ball and reading the future. There's lots of interesting stories told about the legend of Biddy Early.

The Black Rose

160 State Street   617.742.2286

open Mon - Sat 11am 'til 2am,
Sun 9am 'til 2am

Boston's legendary Black Rose, located right next to the Faneuil Hall - Quincy Market area, is the best known Irish pub in Boston and rightly considered one of the best Irish pubs in America. Family-friendly 'til 9pm, then the 21+ crowd takes over.

Food: Kitchen is open daily 11:30am 'til 9pm. The fare features many popular Irish and American specialties. The menu is always evolving and always features fresh and hearty pub food. A great traditional Irish and American breakfast is served Saturday and Sunday 'til Noon.

Entertainment: Live bands 364 nights per year (the only exception is Christmas Eve.). On the weekends there's 2 bands; one upstairs, one downstairs. There's also a couple of TVs at the bar to catch the game.

What's In A Name: The Little Black Rose as it is translated from its original Irish, Rosin Dubh, is one of the more beautiful of the many allegorical names for Ireland. It's taken from a 17th century poem. The "black" refers to Ireland's sometimes tragic history; while "rose" refers to the island's beauty.

Coogan's

173 Milk Street   617.451.7415

open daily 11am 'til 2am

Coogan's is very popular with the Financial District crowd and has a loyal following among those looking for downtown fun on weekends. Among Coogan's many sharp features are beautiful Bavarian banquet tables and comfortable cushion seating. A great place to grab a bite during the summer when they throw open the French windows.

Food: The kitchen is open daily 11:30am 'til 9pm. The menu includes great seafood and prime-cut steaks. There's usually a lobster special. The wine list is extensive.

Entertainment: A DJ gets the crowd at Coogan's moving every Thursday, Friday and Saturday night. They also have an earlier live music "happy hour" on Fridays from 4pm 'til 8pm.

What's In A Name: The pub was originally named Coogan's Bluff, the title of a Clint Eastwood movie. After a renovation the name was shortened to Coogan's.

Irish Famine Memorial

The 25 pubs in this chapter are all within a few minutes walk of the Boston Irish Famine Memorial at the corner of School and Washington Streets. The Memorial was dedicated on June 28, 1998 to commemorate the 150th anniversary of the Irish Famine.

Durty Nelly's

108 Blackstone Street
617.742.2090

open daily 11am 'til 2am

Well they've done it again! The good folks from the Somers Pubs Group have captured the magical allure of a true Irish pub and produced another winner. Situated in the newest "best location" in town, Durty Nelly's has set up shop in the historic Haymarket; a few steps from the Freedom Trail, across the street from the lovely North End and a short stroll from the skyscrapers of Downtown. Nelly's is two fantastic floors of pub perfection. The first floor is comfortable-cozy and overflowing with Irish charm. Large windows open to the beautiful Rose Kennedy Greenway. The second floor takes the form of a luxurious 18th century dining room and offers wonderful views of the city. Outside, sit at their Parisian-like sidewalk café tables and relax to the sounds of the Greenway's fountains. A wonderful lunchtime spot to meet and agree on a deal with an honest handshake. This pub is also the quintessential place to meet after a hectic day and relax with friends, enjoy some good conversation and a delicious stout. A haven for hospitality we are sure that Durty Nelly's will soon be another Boston landmark.

Food: Serving lunch and dinner, good hearty Irish fare including a full Irish Breakfast offered all day. Each evening the dinner menu reinvents itself depending on the season's best and freshest ingredients.

Entertainment: The best live entertainers; regular performers include Mike Barrett (every Sunday night) and special appearances by wonderful artist like Finbar Furey. All the games are covered on multiple TVs.

What's In A Name: John Joe Somers' inspiration for his newest venture came from the memories and stories of his neighbor, Nelly O'Sullivan. Nelly ran a stall at the Quay Market in Cork City, Ireland, where she was always ready with a quick response and a smart piece of wit. Nelly got her name from the old shawl, which she wore day in and day out but never got sight of a washbasin. Her thinking on that being, "Ah sure it'll only get durty again!" The original Durty Nelly's is a famous Irish pub, established in 1620, and located right next to Bunratty Castle in County Clare.

PubCorner.com

Emmets

6 Beacon Street
617.742.8565

open daily 11am 'til 2am

Emmets is a good looking, laid back pub located just down the hill from the State House. Excellent wine selection. This is a great spot for catching the ear of your senator or representative.

Food: Emmets' kitchen, open 'til 11pm, turns out familiar pub favorites such as burgers, Fish & Chips and grilled entrees.

Entertainment: Big screen for watching the games.

What's In A Name: The pub is named after Robert Emmet (1778 - 1803), an Irish nationalist rebel leader who led an abortive rebellion against British rule in 1803. He was captured, tried and beheaded on Thomas Street, Dublin on September 20, 1803.

Goody Glover's

50 Salem Street   617.367.6444

open daily 4pm 'til 1am

The North End's only Irish Pub; Goody Glover's spans two floors and combines a warm-cozy ambience with a fun-friendly attitude. Here you can relax, let your guard down and make new friends. In a neighborhood famous for Italian cuisine, Goody's delicious pub fare offers a welcome change of pace.

Food: Goody's describes its menu as "Pub Bistro" in style. You'll find lots of your traditional favorites done up with a creative touch. A few favorites are the Bangers & Mash, Corned Beef & Cabbage Spring Rolls and the 8oz. Prime Black Angus Burger.

Entertainment: Pub Quiz on Wednesday. Plenty of TVs for watching the games. Goody's may be adding live entertainment at some point in the future.

What's In A Name: The last woman to be hanged in Boston as a witch was Goodwife "Goody" Ann Glover, an Irish laundress who lived in the North End. The infamous Reverend Cotton Mather, pastor of the old North Church, accused her of practicing witchcraft in 1688.

The Grand Canal

57 Canal Street   617.523.1112

open daily 11am 'til 2am

The Grand Canal is one of the finest bar/dining establishments in Boston. This tavern is upscale in design, ambience and service but does not offer a snobby attitude. The pub is divided into three main areas. The main room features a large handsome bar, relaxed lighting and correctly set tables for dining. The second area is to the right of the bar and overlooks it; it's quieter and provides additional white tablecloth dining. Directly beneath is the third region, similar to the space above in décor but providing a view of the main bar from below. Grand Canal is a huge party stop on weekends and is popular place to meet for a pint or a bite before a TD BankNorth Garden event. Catering and private rooms are available for functions and special social events.

Food: The Grand Canal's menu is Irish - American fare with a great appetizer selection. For the full menu please visit www.thegrandcanalboston.com

Entertainment: Trivia on Wednesday. Live music on Friday and Saturday. Three huge HDTV plasmas plus a large projection TV for all the games. Internet satellite music system.

What's In A Name: The pub is named after Ireland's Grand Canal built in the mid 18th century to connect Dublin to the Shannon River, Ireland's longest waterway. Clear water and grain were imported into Dublin through the canal and Guinness was shipped out to the world.

James Michael Curley Statues

Legendary Boston politician James Michael Curley (1874 - 1958), described by author Jack Beatty as the "Rascal King" and the model for Frank Skeffington in Edwin O'Connor's "The Last Hurrah," dominated Boston's political landscape for decades. Aside from holding a number of municipal positions, Curley served a term as a Representative in the Massachusetts Legislature from 1902-03. He served in the US House Of Representatives 1911-14. After congress he set his sights on the mayor's office. Back in those days Boston's mayors weren't

allowed to serve consecutive terms. Curley ran, won and served 4 terms as Boston's mayor from 1914-18, 1922-26 and 1930-34. He then ran for Governor of Massachusetts and won, serving from 1935-37. In 1943 he ran again for the US House Of Representatives and won; serving from 1943-45. Then he capped off his political career by running for mayor of Boston one last time. He won and served as mayor from 1945-49.

The Curley statues are located in the park on Congress Street across from City Hall. Appropriately, the big picture window that overlooks the statues is the mayor's office.

Green Dragon Tavern

11 Marshall Street   617.367.0055

open daily 11am 'til 2am

The Green Dragon Tavern is a comfortable place with a real European atmosphere, cheap eats and 20 imported beers. It is a homey bar that caters to a casual crowd; but don't be surprised if you rub shoulders with a sports star or a famous celebrity in town. Great party atmosphere at night.

Food: The menu features Irish - American cuisine with a good selection of fresh seafood. A traditional Irish breakfast is served Saturdays and Sundays. Lunch and brunch is served 'til 3pm; dinner 'til 9pm. Great appetizer menu.

Entertainment: Cover bands perform Tuesday through Sunday nights. Monday is comedy night.

What's In A Name: The pub is named after the original Green Dragon Tavern, which was a headquarters for revolutionaries in Boston and the place where Paul Revere waited (and maybe had a pint) before receiving his signal from the Old North Church and setting out on his historic ride.

The Harp

85 Causeway Street
617.742.1010

open daily 11am 'til 2am

The Harp is located across the street from the TD BankNorth Garden. It's a great place to grab a bite to eat before a game or other event. The service is always great, but when something is going on across the street they make a special effort to get you your meal quickly so you won't be late.

Food: Lunch is served 11am - 3pm, dinner 3pm - 9pm. The menu is Irish-American fare and is updated often.

Entertainment: Live bands and DJs entertain Thursday through Saturday nights. Most often The Harp will have a band upstairs and a DJ downstairs. They have NFL Sunday Ticket™ on their numerous TVs during the season and lots of fun gameday promotions.

What's In A Name: The harp has been a symbol of Ireland since the time of Brian Boru, who was High King of Ireland from 1002 to 1014 and a harp player. The Brian Boru harp is preserved at Trinity College Dublin and is the harp used as Ireland's national emblem and is depicted on the Guinness logo.

Hennessy's

25 Union Street   617.742.2121

open daily 11am 'til 2am

Named "Best Irish Pub" in Boston by Improper Bostonian magazine. There's a packed house every weekend night. A fireplace lends to the traditional Irish decor in the dining room. Private snugs in the back. Upstairs is Hennessy's "Hooley House," designed in the fashion of an old Irish village pub.

Food: The menu features Irish - American cuisine and serves a great Shepherd's Pie, Fish & Chips, and traditional Beef Stew. Huge appetizer menu.

Entertainment: Live music seven nights a week. The fun starts at 5pm on Fridays with Hennessy's "After Work" party. Wednesday is Karaoke Band night.

What's In A Name: Mr. Hennessy was the "straight man" character to Mr. Dooley in stories by Chicago journalist Peter Finley Dunne.

Hurricane O'Reilly's

150 Canal Street
617.722.0161

open Wed - Fri 11:30am 'til 2am,
Sat 4pm 'til 2am, closed Sun - Tue

Located in the shadows of the TD BankNorth Garden, Hurricane O'Reilly's is a Mardi Gras themed, Irish pub that's a popular pre-game watering hole. On weekend nights the Mardi Gras spirit takes over as the area's best DJs turn this into one of Boston's hottest nightclubs.

Food: Hurricane O'Reilly's serves Creole, Irish and American pub-style fare with a large selection of appetizers, soups, salads, burgers, sandwiches and entrees. The award-winning Clam Chowder is very popular.

Entertainment: DJs entertain Fridays and Saturdays. There's more than a dozen TVs, including a big screen, for watching the games.

What's In A Name: Hurricane O'Reilly's is the name of a famous New Orleans bar.

J.J. Foley's
Bar & Grille

21 Kingston Street   617.338.7713

open Mon - Sat 10am 'til 2am,
closed Sun

Foley's has always been one of the most popular pubs in downtown Boston. It's a place where you'll find bike messengers rubbing shoulders with bankers and lawyers and others from the financial district. A great place to go with your friends or to make some new friends.

Food: The kitchen is open Monday - Friday 11:30am 'til 9pm and Saturday 11am 'til 7pm. The menu is traditional pub fare featuring burgers, sandwiches, salads and grilled entrees.

Entertainment: Foley's has TV and a great jukebox; maybe the best jukebox in the city.

What's In A Name: The pub was opened in 1909 by John Joseph Foley who emigrated to America from Kerry.

José McIntyre's

160 Milk Street   617.451.9460

open daily 11am 'til 2am

José McIntyre's is Boston's only Irish-Mexican cantina and a great escape from the hustle and bustle of the Financial District. It offers 2 floors, 3 bars, and no hassle fun! Great open-air dining and merrymaking during our warmer months when they throw open the windows.

Food: The new menu features the very eclectic mix of authentic Irish cuisine and spicy Mexican dishes. Just imagine, while you're having Mrs. McIntyre's Meatloaf the person across from you may be enjoying a Buffalo Chicken Quesadilla. The full menu is available daily 'til 9pm.

Entertainment: Live bands and DJs entertain every Thursday, Friday and Saturday night. Great dance floor! They have billiards and darts, plenty of TVs and even a shuffleboard court in the back room.

What's In A Name: During the Mexican Civil War quite a few Irishmen went to Mexico to join the freedom fighters. They were nicknamed "José McIntyres." Also, the name celebrates the concept of an "Irish pub with Mexican grub."

Kennedy's Midtown

42 Province Street   617.426.3333

open daily 11am 'til 1am

Kennedy's Midtown is a lively Irish Pub & Steak House with a nice piano and martini bar that hums with the cheerful banter of patrons. One of Boston's best kept secrets, Kennedy's offers all the comforts of a traditional Irish Pub, with a touch of elegance.

Food: Kennedy's has perhaps the most expansive menu of fine fare you'll find at any Irish pub. The cuisine is International and includes all your Irish favorites. The Honey Bourbon Salmon is great. Brunch is served on Sundays.

Entertainment: Live music in the piano bar with styles ranging from Jazz to Rhythm & Blues.

What's In A Name: Kennedy is a good Irish name, especially here in Boston, and the pub is located in Boston's midtown; between Downtown Crossing and the historic Boston Common and just steps from Beacon Hill, the Freedom Trail, Boston's Theatre District and Faneuil Hall.

The Kinsale

2 Center Plaza   617.742.5577

**open Mon & Tue 9am 'til 12:30am,
Wed - Fri 9am 'til 2am,
Sat 10am 'til 2am, Sun 10am 'til 12:30am**

The Kinsale, designed and built in Ireland, is a warm, friendly oasis among the hustle and bustle of the surrounding downtown, City Hall across the street, and the courthouse in back. The large outdoor seating area looking out on City Hall Plaza and passing pedestrians is a great place to enjoy a meal and a pint on a warm day.

Food: The Kinsale's menu includes delicious pub fare and Irish specialties but doesn't stop there. You'll find exceptional offerings from around the world. Fantastic Clam Chowder.

Entertainment: Live music Tuesday, Thursday, Friday and Saturday. Wednesday is Trivia Night.

What's In A Name: The pub is named after the port city of Kinsale, located south of Cork City.

Kitty O'Shea's

131 State Street   617.725.0100

open Mon - Sat 11:30am 'til 2am,
Sun noon 'til 2am

Newly renovated and under new management, Kitty O'Shea's is conveniently located outside Boston's historic Faniuel Hall. The pitch pine floors, which are 200 years old, were imported from a church in Belfast, Ireland. The upstairs bar is an old pulpit from an Irish church and the fireplace was brought over from an historic Georgian home in Dublin. Its comfortable, yet lively atmosphere is a draw for everyone working, visiting or playing in Boston.

Food: Kitty's offers up tremendous pub fare. Great lunch selection of sandwiches and burgers (the Buffalo Chicken Sandwich is fantastic). They do a nice Fish & Chips.

Entertainment: DJs on Friday and Saturday nights.

What's In A Name: Katherine Woods was born in 1846 in Bradwell, Essex, England, the daughter of an English chaplain. At the age of 22 she became the wife of Captain Willie O'Shea whom later became an Irish MP. In 1880 Kitty met Charles Stewart Parnell, an Irish nationalist who led the fight for Irish Home Rule in the 1880s. He is fondly remembered in Irish history as the "Uncrowned King of Ireland." In 1881 Kitty and Parnell began an affair that lasted 10 years and some argue that the affair prevented Irish Home Rule from being granted.

The Last Hurrah

60 School Street   617.227.8600

open daily 11:30am 'til 12:30am

The Last Hurrah is a traditional old-style Boston bar whose walls are adorned with photos of local political heavyweights from bygone eras. They do a brisk lunch trade; and the place fills up with an after-work crowd from the financial district.

Food: The menu at The Last Hurrah is light pub fare with plenty of familiar and welcome choices. The New England Clam "Chowda" is excellent. Save room for the Boston Cream Pie, which was invented at The Parker House in 1856.

Entertainment: TVs for watching sporting events.

What's In A Name: The Last Hurrah is a novel by Edwin O'Connor whose main character, Frank Skeffington, is based upon legendary Boston politician James Michael Curley.

McFadden's

148 State Street   617.227.5100

**open Mon - Sat 11:30am 'til 2am,
closed Sun**

McFadden's is the most dynamic spot in downtown Boston; combining both work and play. Offering great food, crazy nightlife and an exciting place to watch a sports game, the many facets of McFadden's will never disappoint. A constant buzz of activity after 5pm, this bar really comes alive after 9pm offering a wild and crazy scene.

Food: Lunch and dinner. Affordable and of a high quality, perfect for business or pleasure. Salads, Sandwiches (try the "Great 8", your choice from eight large and tasty sandwich plates for only $8). "Legendary" Boneless Wings, Burgers, Ribs, Shepherd's Pie, Fish and Chips, yummy chicken and steak dishes.

Entertainment: DJ's on Thursday, Friday and Saturday playing DJ, Top 40, Hip-Hop, Dance, 70's Disco, 80's, 90's and Reggae. Monday and Wednesday are Rock Acoustic Nights. Ten 42" plasma TV's, a large projection screen TV, and six booths with their own individual TV's to watch all of their sports packages.

What's In A Name: The McFadden's pubs are named after their original location; McFadden's on Second Avenue in New York City.

McGann's

197 Portland Street
617.227.4059

**open Mon - Sat 11:30 'til 2am,
Sun noon 'til 2am**

Since opening his original pub in Ireland, Tommy McGann's mission has been simple: great music, food and endless entertainment. McGann's is best known for its music. The best Irish musicians have performed here including Christy Moore, Donal Lurry, Sinead O'Connor, The Corrs, Luka Bloom and The Saw Doctors.

Food: McGann's offers impressive pub grub in a lovely setting. The Fisherman's Platter is fantastic and sure to fill you up.

Entertainment: Live music Friday and Saturday nights. McGann's shows live broadcasts of all major soccer, gaelic football and rugby matches via satellite.

What's In A Name: Named after its sister pub, McGann's, in Doolin, County Clare, Ireland.

Mr. Dooley's

77 Broad Street   617.338.5656

open each day 11am 'til 2am

Nestled in the heart of Boston's Financial District, Mr. Dooley's is an oasis of down to earth hospitality. They've remained true to honest Irish pub tradition. As one of the bar staff remarked... "If ya want a Theme Park....go to Disney...if ya want a pub....come to Dooley's."

Food: The menu features Irish - American cuisine. An award winning Irish Breakfast is served every Saturday and Sunday. There are always a few specials available for lunch and dinner.

Entertainment: Live Irish entertainment Tuesday through Sunday nights.

What's In A Name: Mister Dooley is a character created by Chicago journalist Finley Peter Dunne in 1893. Set in a South Side Chicago Irish pub, Mr. Dooley, the owner and bartender, would expound upon political and social issues of the day using the thick accent of an Irish immigrant.

Ned Devine's

1 Faneuil Hall Marketplace
617.248.8800

open daily 11am 'til 2am

Located in Quincy Market, Ned Devine's has a huge upstairs pub with a magnificent decor, a small downstairs bar and an outdoor patio. It's a great place for weary tourists to stop in for a bite, a pint, and some Boston "insider tips."

Food: Ned Devine's features an all-day menu of lighter American cuisine with all the familiar Irish favorites.

Entertainment: DJs entertain regularly and there's plenty of TVs for sports fans.

What's In A Name: The pub takes its name from the title character of the 1998 film "Waking Ned Devine," which was set in the fictional Irish village of Tulaigh Mhór (Tullymore) and filmed in and around the village of Cregneash on the Isle of Man.

Paddy O's

33 Union Street   617.263.7771

open each day 11am 'til 2am

Walk through the modest front door and be shocked by the grand scale of Paddy O's Irish Pub. Wonderful cottage country décor, a long handsome bar with plenty of sturdy stools, many private tables and a professional stage with space in front to get down and boogie. Paddy O's comforts with authentic Irish atmosphere, delicious food, great music, and a true Irish staff. Pleasing the eye, ear, stomach and soul.

Food: A marvelous menu, abundant in choice and serving size, petite in price. Fun starters (try the Dublin Crabby Cheese Dunk), Soups and Salads. All the Irish faves, Bangers and Mash, Shepherd's Pie, Ale Battered Fish and Chips, etc. Wonderful fresh seafood dishes. Unique Sandwiches. Gourmet Burgers (Black Angus Beef – Extra Lean). Aged Gourmet Steaks, Black Angus Sterling Quality.

Entertainment: Sensational live music Wednesday through Sunday from Top 40 to rousing Irish ballads. A modern first class sound system and lots of flat screen TVs. The place to meet friends and catch a game.

What's In A Name: The owner named his pub after a wise and interesting friend.

Purple Shamrock

One Union Street   617.227.2060

open Mon - Sat 11am 'til 2am,
Sun 9am 'til 2am

The Purple Shamrock is one of the busiest bars in Boston, Irish or otherwise. It's popular with the locals and a great diversion for tourists visiting Faneuil Hall or strolling Boston's Freedom Trail.

Food: Lunch is served daily 'til 4:30pm, dinner 'til 9pm. The menu is a good selection of Irish and American favorites and features several fresh seafood offerings. A traditional Irish and American breakfast is served Saturday and Sunday 9am 'til noon.

Entertainment: Thursday is Karaoke Night and live bands entertain on Saturdays. A good place to catch the games on TV.

What's In A Name: The pub's name is taken from the title of the autobiography of legendary Boston Mayor and Massachusetts' Governor, the "Rascal King" himself, James Michael Curley. There are two great Curley statues in the park right across from the pub.

The Times

112 Broad Street   617.357.8463

open daily 10am 'til 2am

Not your typical Irish pub. The Times is nestled along the new "greenway" created by the removal of the elevated expressway. It has secured its reputation as a "Post Riverdance Pub" with its great food, wine, beer selection. Terrific outdoor seating area looking out across the new Greenway.

Food: The chef, Mike Oliver, is great. The menu includes a nice selection of American and Irish food including a good variety of New England seafood dishes. The Steak Tips and burgers are very popular. There's always a few good specials on offer. The Times took home the gold medal for their clam chowder in the 2002 Boston Chowderfest.

Entertainment: Live bands on Thursdays. Band or DJ on Fridays and Saturdays. There are two dart boards and the big screen TV shows most major sporting events.

What's In A Name: The Times is named after the newspaper The Irish Times.

Fenway Park

Where you find the craic you're sure to find Guinness, and there's nowhere in Boston where the craic is stronger than at Fenway Park. The grass is green, the famed "Monster" is green, and our beloved World Series Champions even sport green caps each Saint Patrick's Day for a spring training game. This pub-style beer stand, serving Guinness and Smithwick's, is located in the lower concourse behind home plate.

BACK BAY, SOUTH END, KENMORE

An Tua Nua

835 Beacon St.   617.262.2121

open Mon - Wed 11am 'til 1am,
Thu - Sat 11am 'til 2am,
Sun 11am 'til 2am

An Tua Nua is one of Boston's more popular Irish nightspots. It's only a five minute walk from Fenway Park. It's front room is a traditional Irish pub while the huge back room serves as the nightclub, with a lively mix of students and local Irish. The crowd is usually young and attractive.

Food: Served daily 'til 8pm, 7pm on Sundays. New chef and new extensive menu. Tons to choose from. Many fresh seafood and pasta items. The Lunch & Game Day menu features burgers, soups, salads, specialty pizzas and a few entrees. The dinner menu has traditional favorites like Shepherd's Pie and Fish & Chips. The Steak Tips with are out of this world!

Entertainment: A DJ hosts club events in the huge back room every night. Theme nights feature Top 40, Gothic, House, Reggae, Retro and more. Salsa dancing on Wednesdays in the back room. Thursday is College Night with drink specials.

What's In A Name: An Tua Nua means "A New Beginning."

Clery's

113 Dartmouth Street   617.262.9874

open Monday - Saturday 11am 'til 2am,
Sunday 10am 'til 2am

Clery's is a South End landmark and a great respite from shopping at Copley Place, which is located one block away. They have three bars, a fireplace, a lodgeroom and a bistro room for quiet dining. The downstairs "Down Bar" has a dance floor and is open Thursday through Saturday nights providing a club atmosphere.

Food: Clery's menu offers a good sampling of Irish and American favorites. It includes aged Angus steaks, pizzas, and award-winning Clam Chowder. The kitchen is open daily 11:30am 'til midnight. Sunday Brunch is served 10am 'til 3pm.

Entertainment: A DJ entertains every Thursday, Friday and Saturday night. Wednesday Trivia Night. You can always catch your favorite sporting event on the TV at Clery's.

What's In A Name: The pub is named after the famous Clery's department store on O'Connell Street in Dublin. The clock outside Clery's is a popular meeting place. Folks will often plan to "meet at Clery's clock."

Conor Larkin's

329 Huntington Avenue
617.867.0084

open Mon - Sat 11:30am 'til 1am,
Sunday Noon 'til 1am

Conor Larkin's is a very popular hangout for Northeastern University students. The low ceiling adds to the cozy feeling of this tidy pub. The $7 pitchers are an indication of how inexpensive this pub is. "Cheap beer and great food" is the way they do it here.

Food: Conor Larkin's serves up very tasty pub grub. Full menu including Fish & Chips and Shepherd's Pie. The pastas are excellent. For veggie lovers, try the Portobello Sandwich. The Steak Tips are great and there's always a few daily specials.

Entertainment: Pub Quiz on Tuesday. They also have a jukebox and 6 satellite TVs.

What's In A Name: Conor Larkin is a fictional character and the chief protagonist in Leon Uris' novel, Trinity.

Crossroads Irish Pub

495 Beacon Street   617.262.7371

open daily 11am 'til 2am

Crossroads is the oldest Irish pub in the Back Bay. It has operated under the name Crossroads since 1963. It has two floors. The downstairs is a relaxing pub atmosphere and serves as the dining area. Upstairs gets lively at night with a mix of students from Boston University and M.I.T. and young professionals from the neighborhood.

Food: The kitchen is open 'til midnight each day. The menu consists of burgers, sandwiches, pizzas and traditional pub style entrees. There are always a few daily specials. On Wednesday nights buy a pitcher of beer and get a free pizza.

Entertainment: Crossroads has 4 dart boards, a jukebox and Golden Tee Golf. On Saint Patrick's Day entertainment is provided by an Irish band.

What's In A Name: The pub is located at the major crossroads of Massachusetts Avenue and Beacon Street. Crossroads is a common name for pubs in Ireland.

Cuffs

154 Berkeley St.   617.532.3827

open Mon - Sat 11am 'til 2am,
Sun 10am 'til 2am

The bar of the new Jury's Hotel, Cuffs is a sharp-looking space with a light-hearted atmosphere and a Boston Police themed decor. They boast one of the best outdoor terraces in Boston and a wonderful, warm fireplace.

Food: Cuffs offers top-quality bar fare along with some traditional favorites. The Pulled Pork Sandwich, Grilled Flatbread Pizza and Lobster Roll are among the favorites.

Entertainment: Several TVs.

What's In A Name: Jury's Hotel is located in the old Boston Police Headquarters and "Cuffs" is short for handcuffs...or cufflinks, depending on your mood.

J.J. Foley's Café

117 East Berkeley St.   617.728.9101

open Mon - Sat 9am 'til 2am,
Sun Noon 'til 2am

Foley's is a Boston institution and long favored watering hole for politicians and journalists. It is the oldest family run bar in Boston. Big space with two separate bar rooms.

Food: Foley's offers a traditional pub menu of soups, sandwiches, burgers and a selection of familiar entrees. Brunch on Sunday.

Entertainment: Foley's has TVs and a dart board and hosts dart leagues on Tuesday nights. Video games available in back.

What's In A Name: The pub is named after the owner's great-grandfather, Jeremiah Foley, who emigrated to Boston from County Kerry and established the pub in 1909.

Lir

903 Boylston Street
617.778.0089

open daily 11:30am 'til 1am

Lir is more accurately described as a Dublin pub rather than an Irish pub. Downstairs is more lounge-like while the upstairs bar, reached via a spiral staircase, is more elegant. Good beer selection.

Food: Lir's menu includes Irish and pub favorites. The Dublin Steak Tips are great. They also make a heck of a pizza pie.

Entertainment: 21 TVs for all you sports lovers. English Premier League games are shown weekend mornings.

What's In A Name: In Irish mythology, Lir ("the sea") was "God of the Sea."

M.J. O'Connor's

27 Columbus Ave.   617.482.2255

open Mon - Sat 11am 'til 2am,
Sun 10am 'til 2am

M.J. O'Connor's is located in the Boston Park Plaza Hotel, one block from The Boston Common. A very convenient location for visitors looking to take a break from walking the Freedom Trail or shopping in the Back Bay.

Food: Lunch is served Monday through Friday 11am - 3pm. Dinner is served 3pm - 11pm Monday through Saturday, 2pm - 10pm on Sundays. O'Connor's serves a terrific Sunday Brunch from 10am 'til 2pm. The menu is best described as "Irish-Eclectic." It features Shepherd's Pie, Tri-Color Soup (green, white and orange of course!), fresh steaks and seafood, and a lush breakfast.

Entertainment: Live Irish Seisiún performances are featured on various nights at M.J. O'Connor's. Call for information.

What's In A Name: The pub is named after the owner's father, Michael Joseph O'Connor.

Solas

710 Boylston Street   617.933.4803

open daily 11am 'til 2am

Located in the Lenox Hotel and across from the historic Boston Public Library, Solas is a great compliment to Boston's Back Bay scene. They offer two floors of fun; each with its own bar and dining area. Great French windows open onto busy Boylston Street during the warmer months.

Food: Solas has an impressive menu that offers up tasty pub food with some familiar Irish favorites. The Irish Mac & Cheese with smoked ham and Irish cheddar are excellent.

Entertainment: Live bands upstairs on Monday and Tuesday nights. TVs for watching the games.

What's In A Name: Solas means "comfort" in Gaelic.

ALLSTON, BRIGHTON, BROOKLINE

The Boyne

458 Western Avenue, Brighton
617.782.2418

open Mon - Sat 8am 'til 2am,
Sun 11am - 2am

The Boyne is one of the few pubs in Boston where parking is available. They also have a private function room available for parties. You'll be pleasantly surprised by the wallet friendly prices at The Boyne.

Food: The Boyne's kitchen serves lunch only Monday through Thursday 11am 'til 3pm, Friday 11am 'til 9pm, Saturday 11am 'til 5pm, and Sunday 11am 'til 3pm. It has a typical pub menu of sandwiches, burgers and grilled entrees. Irish Breakfast and Mixed Grilled is served daily and there are also daily specials such as Fish & Chips, London Broil, Roast Pork and Roast Turkey.

Entertainment: Video DJs and Karaoke on Friday and Saturday nights. There are dart boards and a jukebox.

What's In A Name: The pub is named after the River Boyne in County Meath.

Castlebar

575 Washington Street, Brighton
617.783.5722

open daily 10am 'til 1am

Castlebar is a popular pub in the Oak Square section of Brighton. They attract a lively and diverse mix of grad students, young professionals and colorful local characters. The large, open lounge area is great for events, parties and meetings.

Food: Cheeseburgers and Fries are available Monday through Friday noon 'til 10:30pm.

Entertainment: There's a couple of dart boards along with Golden Tee Golf and Big Buck Hunter video games. Pub Quiz on Thursday nights. Live music Friday nights.

What's In A Name: Though the original proprietor was a Roscommon man, he always enjoyed the song "Take Me Back To Castlebar" in the County of Mayo. This is the third pub he'd been involved with and all were named after his favorite song titles.

Maurice Tobin

Maurice Joseph Tobin (1901-53), a son of immigrants from Clogheen, Tipperary, entered politics as a protege of the legendary James Michael Curley, winning a seat in the Massachusetts House of Representatives at the age of 25, serving 1927-29. He served on the Boston School Committee 1931-37 before shocking the political establishment by defeating Curley in the 1937 race for Mayor of Boston. He served as Mayor 1938-45. In 1944 Tobin was elected Governor and served two years, 1945-47. Upon Harry Truman's election as president, Tobin was appointed as U.S. Secretary of Labor, a position he held 1948-53.

In 1967, the Mystic River Bridge was renamed the Maurice J. Tobin Memorial Bridge.

This statue of Maurice Tobin on the Charles River Esplanade, in front of the Hatch Shell.

Common Ground

85 Harvard Avenue, Allston
617.783.2071

open daily Noon 'til 2am

The Common Ground Pub has a cool laid-back atmosphere during the afternoon and early evening, making it a great place to "de-stress" after a long day. Later at night and on weekends it tends to become quite a bit more lively, a true party spot. This pub has a handsome and cozy interior with lots of dark woods, plenty of seating and a grand bar. The main room also serves as the dance floor when bands perform or the DJ spins. There's a pleasant little patio available, a great place to hang during warm weather. At Common Ground a cool levelheaded staff and attractive unpretentious customers help add to the wonderful informal atmosphere.

Food: Great pub menu featuring burgers, steaks, pizzas, wings and all the familiar favorites. They were named among the "Great 8" by the Phantom Gourmet for their burgers. The Irish Pizza and Guinness Beef Stew are two popular choices.

Entertainment: Stump Team Trivia on Monday. Guitar Hero (open to all) on Wednesday. DJ Brian All-80's Love Night on Thursday. Bands and DJs entertain on Friday and Saturday (Fri features 90's music). NFL Sunday Ticket. Free WiFi service. All the major American and international sporting events on many TVs.

What's In A Name: The pub is named after the book Common Ground by J. Anthony Lukas which is about Boston during the turbulent decade of the 70s. The story is told through the experiences of three families.

Mayor Kevin White

Born in Jamaica Plain, Kevin Hagan White (1929-) is the longest serving Mayor of Boston, holding the office 1968-84.

This statue, dedicated in 2007, stands across from City Hall and right in front of Faneuil Hall.

Corrib Pub

396 Market Street, Brighton
617.787.0882

open Mon - Sat 8am 'til 1am,
Sun 10am 'til 1am

The Corrib, located in Brighton Center, is the oldest Irish pub in Brighton; opened by the Bligh family in 1969. It's been a longtime favorite among the local Irish who enjoy its home cooking and relaxing atmosphere.

Food: The kitchen is open 11am 'til 10pm each day. They serve the usual pub fare of soups, salads and sandwiches along with a wide-ranging selection of beef, chicken, pasta and seafood entrees. The Corrib's Roast Beef is incredible. A traditional Irish Breakfast is served Saturday and Sunday.

Entertainment: The Corrib, being a pub where people go to enjoy the companionship of their fellow patrons, doesn't offer much in the way of diversions. There's a jukebox and TVs at the bar.

What's In A Name: Like its sister pubs in Brookline and West Roxbury, the Corrib Pub is named after Lough Corrib, a lake in County Galway.

Corrib Pub

201 Harvard Street, Brookline
617.232.8787

open Mon - Sat 8am 'til 1am,
Sun Noon 'til 1am

The Corrib, just a 10 minute walk from the birthplace of John Fitzgerald Kennedy, was opened in 1973 and has developed a loyal clientele among the locals. The Corrib is more a restaurant than a bar.

Food: The kitchen is open 'til 10pm each day offering authentic Irish Pub Home Cooking. They serve the usual pub fare of soups, salads and sandwiches along with a wide-ranging selection of beef, chicken, pasta and seafood entrees. The Corrib's Irish Mixed Grill is a favorite.

Entertainment: For patrons of The Corrib the entertainment is each other's company. There are TVs at the bar.

What's In A Name: Like its sister pubs in Brighton and West Roxbury, the Corrib Pub is named after Lough Corrib, a lake in County Galway.

Devlin's

332 Washington St.   617.779.8822

open daily 10am 'til 1am

They say Delvin's is "a little bit of downtown, uptown." It's an affordable and casual fine dining establishment which has developed a loyal legion of customers who visit morning, noon and night. They have a wonderful outdoor patio area with seating for 50.

Food: Devlin's offers some of the best dining in the Allston-Brighton area. The menu includes contemporary American steak, seafood and pork dishes along with gourmet pizzas. Sunday Brunch is served 'til 3pm and the highlight of this fantastic breakfast is Devlin's tremendous omelettes.

Entertainment: DJs entertain Thursday through Saturday nights. Occasionally they'll have a live band in, but only for a special event they'll promote.

What's In A Name: Devlin is the family name of one of the owners.

The Green Briar

304 Washington Street, Brighton
617.789.4100

open daily 11am 'til 1am

The Green Briar is located in the heart of Brighton Center, but known citywide as one of Boston's most exciting pubs. A friendly, well trained staff will help you relax and savor this genuine Irish setting. This is a favored pub for international sports fans and a true hot-spot for live entertainment. There are two huge function rooms available for parties and the spacious patio is popular during the summer.

Food: Lunch is served 11am - 4pm, dinner 4pm - 10pm. Appetizers are available 'til 11pm. The menu includes favorites such as Shepherd's Pie, Bangers & Mash, Irish Stout Onion Soup, a Taste Of Ireland Appetizer Sampler and Irish Breakfast (served all day!). Great Sunday Brunch.

Entertainment: Entertainment at The Green Briar runs the full gamut. There's live entertainment each evening featuring a DJ, Boston's best live bands, traditional Irish seisiún and trivia contests. Most major international sporting events are shown live on a huge projection TV.

What's In A Name: The name refers to the briar patches which cover Ireland.

Irish Village

224 Market Street, Brighton
617.787.5427

open daily Noon 'til 1am

The Irish Village has been gaining a reputation as one of the city's best and most authentic Irish pubs. Cozy and comfortable, with a hint of elegance; this is a traditional Irish pub with a very friendly atmosphere.

Food: No kitchen; or, as they said when we asked about the food: "Yeah, Guinness. Food for the soul."

Entertainment: The Irish Village is very popular with soccer fans, as most major international matches are shown live on their TVs. There's a dart board and The Irish Village is the home pub of two dart teams.

What's In A Name: The Irish Village is typical of many of the pubs you'll find in the villages across the Irish countryside.

54th Regiment Memorial

This bronze relief honoring the all black Massachusetts 54th Infantry in the Civil War was created by Augustus Saint Gaudens (1848-1907) who is considered America's greatest 19th century sculptor. Gaudens was born on Charlemont Street in Dublin at the height of the Irish Famine and his family emigrated to Boston when he was 6 months old.

The memorial, dedicated in 1878, is located on the Freedom Trail across from the State House at the entrance to the Boston Common.

Joshua Tree

1316 Commonwealth Ave., Allston
617.566.6699

open Mon - Wed 5pm 'til 1am,
Thu & Fri 5pm 'til 2am, Sat 10am 'til 1am

The newest addition to the Joshua Tree group is a large modern "sports-nightclub." Here they focus on a unique menu and complete sports coverage. This pub is one huge open space divided into distinct areas for dining, socializing and watching the game with the nucleus being a sizable oval bar. Interesting contemporary lighting, furnishing and fixtures are more reminiscent of what's happening in present-day Dublin than a traditional Irish pub. Because of experienced ownership and the professional management team we are positive the Allston Joshua Tree will soon be a Comm. Ave. landmark.

Food: A full fashionable pub menu offering salads, sandwiches, wraps, interesting burgers, pizzas, eclectic entrees and a special "South Of The Border" section with Mexican dishes. Breakfast served until 3pm on Saturday. All-You-Can-Eat Football Brunch Buffet on Sundays 'til 3pm.

Entertainment: Pool table. An awesome sound system. Lots of plasma TVs and a few big projection screens. Monday is Monday Night Football & Free Pool. Tuesday Trivia with prizes at 8pm. Wednesday 1/2 Price Burger Night. Thursday 80's Rock Night. Friday Boston's Best Music. Saturday Boston's Best Music and College Football. Sunday Football Brunch & Bloody Mary Bar Trivia with prizes at 8pm.

What's In A Name: The pub is named after Joshua Tree National Park in the southwest United States. Joshua Tree was also the name of an album by Ireland's own U2.

James Brendan Connolly

James Brendan Bennet Connolly (1868-1957) of South Boston was the first modern Olympic champion, winning the Triple Jump at the 1896 Olympics in Athens.

This statue of Connolly is located next to the athletic field at Moakley Park in South Boston.

The Kells

161 Brighton Avenue, Allston
617.782.9082

open Mon - Fri 4pm 'til 2am,
Sat and Sun 11am 'til 2am

The Kells has evolved over the past 14 years from a more traditional Irish pub into what is now one of the most popular dance clubs in the city among college students and 20-somethings. They haven't completely strayed from their Irish heritage though. True to their traditional roots, they still pour one of the best pints of Guinness and you can still catch all your favorite international sporting matches here.

Food: The Kells features Asian cuisine and the menu is quite extensive. A couple of good choices are the Moo Shi Chicken and the Crispy Orange Beef.

Entertainment: Beirut League on Mondays. DJ Tuesday through Sunday. Ladies Night on Friday. Plenty of TVs for watching the games.

What's In A Name: The pub gets its name from the famous Book Of Kells, which was written in 800 AD by a team of Irish monks at the Scriptorium of Iona. It took 30 years to complete, contains the four gospels, and is one of the most beautifully illuminated manuscripts.

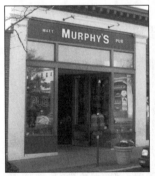

Matt Murphy's Pub

14 Harvard Street, Brookline
617.232.0188

open daily 11:30am 'til 2am

Matt Murphy's is a top-notch restaurant nestled in a cozy, authentic Irish pub. The intimacy of this Brookline Village treasure allows for a true appreciation of a good pint, intellectual conversation and their traditional irish seisiúns. They also serve up some of the best food in the city and have received rave reviews from several major papers for both their great food and atmosphere.

Food: Served daily 'til 10pm. The menu offerings include hearty soups such as their Oxtail Onion, great sandwiches such as the very filling Hot Roast Pork with Pickled Cabbage Slaw, and mouth watering entrees such as the succulent Slow Roasted Duck.

Entertainment: Irish Seisiún entertains on Thursdays and during Sunday Brunch. There's live music every night except Wednesday with no cover charge. Table Quiz is played on Wednesdays.

What's In A Name: The pub's owner named it after her children's grandfather.

O'Brien's

3 Harvard Avenue, Allston
617.782.6245

open daily Noon 'til 1am

The recently renovated O'Brien's, which bills itself as "Allston's oldest surviving rock club," is a cozy "Rock City" tavern providing a venue for local and national acts. O'Brien's has been a springboard for hundreds of artists over the years and through diverse booking and dedicated promotion this tradition is going strong.

Food: No kitchen.

Entertainment: Live bands every night. There's 2 TVs for watching the games; plus cribbage.

What's In A Name: The original owner was named O'Brien, but that was long ago.

O'Leary's

1010 Beacon Street, Brookline
617.734.0049

open Mon - Sat 11:30am 'til 1am,
Sun 4pm 'til 1am

On the Boston - Brookline line and only a 10 minute walk to Fenway Park, O'Leary's is a great alternative to the crowded sports bars before a Sox game. The food, service and hospitality are outstanding. After one visit you'll understand why O'Leary's has developed such a loyal clientele.

Food: O'Leary's menu is a mixed offering of pub favorites and generous entrees. Favored choices include the stews, pot pies and Fish & Chips.

Entertainment: Live acoustic folk performers Wednesday through Saturday. A traditional Irish seisiún entertains on Sundays.

What's In A Name: The pub is named after its owner Aengus O'Leary. Aengus is one of the coolest guys in the city. Stop by and say "hello."

Porter Belly's

338 Washington Street, Brighton
617.254.3300

open daily 11am 'til 1am

The interior and exterior of Porter Belly's is one of the most unique in the Boston area. The intimate lighting, elm-wood finish and fireplace provide the perfect setting for conversation and meeting new friends.

Food: Porter Belly's menu includes familiar pub appetizers and burgers, burgers, burgers. Over 25 different takes on the burger. Try The Dubliner; with cured Irish bacon and Tipperary Cheddar.

Entertainment: Open Mic on Wednesdays. DJ on Thursdays. Karaoke on Sundays.

What's In A Name: A "Porter Belly" is an old Irish term for a beer-belly.

Washington Square Tavern

714 Washington Street, Brookline
617.232.8989

open daily 5pm 'til 2am

The Washington Square Tavern is one of the area's gems. It is immensely popular with young adults from the neighborhood who speak with equal passion about the good food, great beer, excellent wine and cocktails and pleasant, laid-back atmosphere. The chef is Boston native Paul Hathaway.

Food: Dinner is served Sunday through Thursday 'til 10pm, Friday and Saturday 'til 11pm. The menu is contemporary American with a New England flair. You'll never get bored with the menu. It changes every 6 to 8 weeks and is always creative. Brunch is served on Sundays.

Entertainment: The Washington Square Tavern is about dining and socializing and they don't offer any diversions from what their patrons love about the place.

What's In A Name: The pub is located in Washington Square, Brookline.

CAMBRIDGE

The Asgard

350 Massachusetts Avenue
617.577.9100

open Mon - Wed 11am 'til 1am,
Thu & Fri 11am 'til 2am
Sat 10am 'til 2am, Sun 10am 'til 1am

The interior of The Asgard was designed and built in Ireland. Much of the wood used is over 150 years old. The pub's style is medevial-Irish with a Viking influence. The bar area is very lively; the dining area relaxed. This is a comfy, cool pub; the perfect place for relaxing with friends. Private party area for functions.

Food: The cuisine features incredible Irish specialties and creative American cuisine. The full menu is served 'til midnight on weekends. Appetizers are available 'til midnight every day. Some great choices are the Shepherd's Pie, Guinness Steak and Fenian Chicken Pasta.

Entertainment: Live bands entertain Tuesday through Saturday. Tuesday is also Pub Trivia Night. Plenty of TVs for watching your favorite sports.

What's In A Name: The Asgard was a boat made famous for running guns for the Irish Volunteers in 1914.

The Druid

1357 Cambridge St.   617.497.0965

open daily 11am 'til 1am

Located in the oldest wooden mercantile building in Cambridge, The Druid is a cozy pub with antique furnishings and original artwork. Known nationwide as one of America's best Irish pubs, The Druid is the perfect place for a pint and a chat. As they say; "The Druid is what a true Irish pub should be, a great social experience."

Food: Familiar, pub-style menu with lunch and dinner served each day. Brunch and Irish Breakfast served on Saturday and Sunday.

Entertainment: Traditional Irish music on Friday evenings at 6:00. DJ on Thursday and Saturday. Plus there's always cool music flowing from The Druid's sound system. On Wednesdays The Druid hosts perhaps the best Pub Quiz in the city.

What's In A Name: Druids were the high priests of the Celts.

The Field

20 Prospect Street
617.354.7345

open Sun - Wed Noon 'til 1am,
Thu - Sat Noon 'til 2am

The Field is a quaint, authentic Irish bar with a native Irish staff. The decor features Irish antiques and artifacts. This is a great neighborhood pub with a fantastic mix of customers, including university students, colorful characters and local Irish. In business for over 10 years; the owners attribute their success to the relaxed atmosphere, terrific service, and eclectic crowd.

Food: Traditional pub grub is available Monday through Saturday. Lunch is noon 'til 3pm; dinner is 5pm 'til 9pm.

Entertainment: The Field has a pool table and dart boards and there's always great music playing on the jukebox. Plasma TVs cover all the sporting matches.

What's In A Name: The pub is named after the book The Field by John B. Keane which was made into a movie starring Richard Harris.

Grafton Street

1230 Massachusetts Avenue
617.497.0400

open daily 11am 'til 2am

Grafton Street is a smart looking pub with soft lighting and a slate and wood decor. Wonderful French windows on 2 sides. Huge selection of single malt scotches.

Food: Grafton Street's menu is a combination of traditional Irish pub and contemporary American cuisine. Their award-winning brunch, which includes Irish Breakfast, is served on Sunday.

Entertainment: DJs entertain on Thursday and Friday. Live bands on Saturday. There are TVs at the bar for watching the games.

What's In A Name: Grafton Street is a main shopping street in Dublin Centre, running from Saint Stephen's Green in the south to College Green in the north. The street was named after the first Duke of Grafton, who owned land in the area.

People's Republik

876 Massachusetts Ave. 617.491.6969

open Mon - Wed Noon 'til 1am,
Thu - Sun Noon 'til 2am

The People's Republik is an Irish bar with a commie twist. The decor includes many posters saluting communist luminaries and a giant combat boot made from melted LPs. And, yes; that's Elvis in a Soviet Army cap on the outside mural. There's a great 8' x 4' rendition of The Last Supper done by a local artist depicting many People's Republik regulars. The bar attracts a lot of locals from Harvard and Central Squares, including students from Harvard and MIT and the occasional Nobel Prize winner. The crowd is artistic but not pretentious.

Food: Excellent pub grub options. There several specials each day. The Cuban Sandwiches and Cajun Burgers are very popular.

Entertainment: Three dart boards, TV, sound system (bartender's choice on the playlist). Live bands entertain occasionally.

What's In A Name: The name is a homage the City of Cambridge, which is often referred to as "The People's Republic Of Cambridge" due to its left-leaning denizens.

Phoenix Landing

512 Massachusetts Avenue
617.576.6260

open daily 11am 'til 2am

Phoenix Landing is a relaxed bar and restaurant which offers great food at great prices. After 10pm it turns into a very lively nightclub. If you want to party; this is your place.

Food: Phoenix Landing's menu is eclectic American-Irish with daily specials and great desserts. The burgers are very popular; we recommend the Lil Lamb Burger. Sunday brunch is served 'til 3pm. They serve a great Irish Breakfast Saturday and Sunday 'til 3pm.

Entertainment: International soccer and rugby matches are shown on the TVs. There is a 100 CD jukebox. DJs entertain every night to a different theme, ranging from disco, reggae, house & techno, 80s and more.

What's In A Name: The pub is named after the legendary Phoenix, a mythical and sacred firebird in ancient Phoenician mythology.

The Plough & Stars

912 Massachusetts Ave.   617.576.0032

open Sun - Wed 11am 'til 1am,
Thu - Sat 11am 'til 2am

The beloved Plough & Stars attracts all types, from writers, poets and musicians to tradesmen and business people to students and professors from nearby M.I.T. and Harvard University. If you're strolling down Mass. Ave. you're sure to be drawn by the sounds of laughter drifting from its door.

Food: Lunch served daily 'til 2:30pm and a great brunch on Saturday and Sunday. A Cuban Sandwich is offered daily. They have a good selection of soups and some of the more popular entrees include the Stuffed Catfish Filet and the Chicken Confit Pot Pie. Sunday nights is Brendan's Chicken & Fish Fry. Outstanding value across the whole menu.

Entertainment: Live music nightly from 9pm 'til 1am - everything from blues to rock to country to sounds that must be experienced because we can't describe them.

What's In A Name: The pub is loosely named after the play The Plough & The Stars by Sean O'Casey.

Redline

59 JFK Street · 617.491.9851

open Sun - Wed 4pm 'til 1am,
Thurs - Sat 4pm 'til 2am

Redline is a stylish bar in a great location. It's really caught the attention of hip young revelers over the past few years as a place that always provides a memorable night out. Great selection of beer, wine, and specialty cocktails.

Food: Redline's cuisine ranges from All-American favorites to the culturally creative. There are entrees like the 16 oz. T-bone Steak and Fresh Fried Native Cod to a large assortment of sandwiches, appetizers and salads. It's comfort food, and it's very reasonably priced.

Entertainment: Trivia on Mondays. Tuesdays is iPod Night; bring in your iPod and take your turn providing the music. DJs Wednesday through Saturday. 2 TVs at the bar.

What's In A Name: The pub takes its name from the nearby Red Line of the MBTA's subway system.

River Gods

125 River Street · 617.576.1881

open daily 3pm 'til 1am

River Gods is a new-age Irish pub with a unique decor of church pews and Irish antiques arranged to create a modern, hip ambiance. Candles and calm lighting add to the vibe. Terrific barstaff.

Food: River Gods features funky food at moderate prices. Some organic dishes available. The menu might best be described as Irish with an Asian influence. Kitchen closes at 10pm.

Entertainment: Some of the best DJs in the city entertain seven nights a week with styles ranging from R & B to Funk, Soul, Reggae, Brit Pop, Alternative and Rock & Roll.

What's In A Name: The River Gods were ancient deities thought to rule the rivers of Ireland. Also, this pub is located on River Street, just down the street from the Charles River, and the owner, Jackie Linnane, wanted the word "God" in her pub's name.

Shay's

58 JFK Street   617.864.9161

open Mon - Sat 11am 'til 1am,
Sun Noon 'til 1am

Shay's is Harvard Square's coolest pub. It attracts a good mix of students, artists, and locals. The tiny outdoor patio (about the same size as the inside) gets packed on warm, sunny days. Beer and wine only.

Food: Shay's prides itself on good cheap eats. The menu is a pub lover's delight; with excellent burger and sandwich choices. The hand-cut fries are fantastic.

Entertainment: Just television. The bartender is usually playing some good tunes.

What's In A Name: Legend has it that the pub's original owner named Shay's after his lovely daughter, who was said to be blessed with an abundance of Irish luck.

Spirit

2046 Mass. Ave. · 617.868.1555

open Mon - Thu 3pm 'til 1am,
Fri - Sun 11am 'til 1am

Spirit is a really handsome pub with lots of attention to detail. It's tastefully decorated with photos from local photographers, slanted mirrors, comfy booths, and breezy French windows. They have 15 beers on tap plus a good selection of scotches and an interesting martini list. Very popular with sports fans; they really know how to cater to the sports crowd.

Food: The menu at Spirit is described as high-end bar food. Good selection of seafood choices. Irish Breakfast and brunch are served Sundays.

Entertainment: There are 8 big TVs for watching sports. Jukebox and Trivia video game.

What's In A Name: The name alludes to the haunting but peaceful vibe that exists at this pub.

Temple Bar

1688 Massachusetts Avenue
617.547.5055

open Mon - Fri 5pm 'til 1am,
Sat & Sun 10:30am 'til 1am

A casually sophisticated neighborhood bistro, Temple Bar is warm and welcoming. Accented by exposed brick, oversized mirrors, unique lighting and oak paneling, the decor sets a mood you'll enjoy. The bar, which is covered in copper, is truly a work of art. Great late night lounge scene.

Food: Temple bar offers modern American seasonal cuisine focusing on the flavors of New England. Brunch served on Saturday and Sunday. The wine selection is terrific.

Entertainment: Background music provided by a great sound system.

What's In A Name: Temple Bar is a neighborhood on the south bank of the River Liffey in central Dublin. It is Dublin's cultural quarter, has a lively nightlife and has preserved its medieval street pattern, with many narrow cobbled streets. It was named for Sir William Temple, who was provost of Trinity College in the early 17th century and lived in the area.

Cambridge Famine Memorial

The Irish Famine Memorial on Cambridge Common was dedicated on July 23, 1997 by Irish President Mary Robinson.

Tommy Doyle's

96 Winthrop Street
617.864.0655

open Thu - Sat 11am 'til 2am,
Sun - Wed 11am 'til 1am

Tommy Doyle's is located in a most desirable location, right in the center of Harvard Square in the old House of Blues. Three floors of fun, and each with its own bar so you'll never wait for a drink. Dining is also offered on all three floors with plenty of tables and booths. The gang from Tommy Doyle's knows how to run a wonderful pub; this public house lives up to expectations.

Food: Tommy Doyle's has an excellent and diverse menu. Some favorites include the Donegal Scallops, Ma McGrath's Irish Stew and the Black Angus Burgers. Brunch is served Saturday and Sunday 'til 4pm.

Entertainment: Wednesday is Pub Quiz followed by Karaoke. Thursday through Saturday is a live band followed by a DJ. Plenty of TVs for watching the games.

What's In A Name: Tommy Doyle is a famous Kerry footballer that has earned seven All Ireland medals and captained the team in the 1986 final. One of the pub's owners is a good friend of Tommy Doyle.

Tommy Doyle's

One Kendall Square · 617.225.0888

open daily 11am 'til 1am

Tommy Doyle's is a lively pub with a huge, beautiful patio located in the One Kendall Square complex. This is a great place to stop for a drink or a bite after a movie at the Kendall Square Theatre.

Food: Tommy Doyle's has an excellent and diverse menu. Some favorites include the West Cork Fish & Chips, Pulled Pork Sandwich and the Black Angus Burgers. Brunch is served Saturday and Sunday.

Entertainment: Pub Quiz on Tuesdays. DJ on Fridays. All the big foreign matches are shown on their TVs.

What's In A Name: Tommy Doyle is a famous Kerry footballer who has earned seven All Ireland medals and captained the team in the 1986 final. One of the pub's owners is a good friend of Tommy Doyle.

SOMERVILLE

The Burren

247 Elm Street   617.776.6896

open Mon - Fri 11:30am 'til 1am,
Sat & Sun 10am 'til 1am

The Burren captures the rich old-world feel of an Irish pub. The front pub is a great place to gather in the warmth of good friends for a bite, a pint and the joy of companionship. The large back room is one of the best music venues in the city for traditional Irish music.

Food: The kitchen is open each day 'til 9:45pm. The Burren offers great pub fare. The Beer Battered Fish & Chips are very popular. Brunch and Irish Breakfast are served Saturday and Sunday 'til 3pm.

Entertainment: Live traditional music is performed every night at The Burren. Every Monday is Set Dancing Night. No need to be shy if you're a beginner; all are welcome. WiFi internet access.

What's In A Name: The Burren, a great rocky expanse in County Clare, is one of the world's truly unique places.

The Independent

75 Union Square   617.440.6022

open Mon - Thu 4:30pm 'til 1am,
Fri & Sat 4pm 'til 2am,
Sun Noon 'til 1am

The Independent offers "constancy in the midst of inevitable change." Theirs is some of the finest dining in Metropolitan Boston. The Independent's pub area is separate from the more sophisticated dining room. Isolating each space works well; the merry-makers in the pub don't disturb the patrons in the dining room. Everything at The Independent, from service to sustinence, is done right.

Food: The Independent serves a very creative European Bistro menu. Unique, interesting and delicious dishes made with the finest and freshest ingredients. The menu is constantly evolving so remember to visit often.

Entertainment: The relaxed atmosphere and consistently good food and good times are what people come to The Independent for. Accordingly there are no bands, jukebox or distractions.

What's In A Name: Named in honor of Somerville's Prospect Hill, where the first American Flag was raised during the War for Independence and which looms protectively behind The Independent.

Joshua Tree

256 Elm Street   617.623.9910

open Mon - Fri 11:30am 'til 1am,
Sat & Sun 10:30am 'til 1am

Joshua Tree is a cosmopolitan Irish bar located in Somerville's popular Davis Square. They cater to a mix of locals, young people from the city, and students from nearby Tufts University.

Food: Served daily 'til 10pm. Great nightly specials. A popular choice from the menu is the Tips Trio, featuring steak, turkey and ribs. There are over 100 menu items. A great brunch is served Sundays 'til 3pm.

Entertainment: A DJ entertains Thursday through Saturday nights. Live acoustic on Thursdays. Sporting events are shown on the eleven TVs, including a big screen. Background music is provided by Joshua Tree's state of the art satellite sound system.

What's In A Name: The pub is named after Joshua Tree National Park in the southwest United States. Joshua Tree was also the name of an album by Ireland's own U2.

Olde Magoun's Saloon

518 Medford Street   617.776.2600

open daily 11am 'til 1am

Olde Magoun's is a trendy, modern pub that pays proper respect to tradition. The tin ceiling is original; there's a fireplace; and lots of great quotes painted on the walls. They pour a great pint of Guinness and offer a nice assortment of seasonal beers and ales. Ample free parking.

Food: The kitchen at Olde Magoun's offers up some great pub grub. They just might serve the best burgers and Fish & Chips in Somerville. The Chicken Curry and Grilled Mediterranean Pizza are two good menu choices..

Entertainment: Team Trivia on Tuesday. They have all the sports packages for your viewing pleasure and boast a great HDTV set up.

What's In A Name: The pub is named after Magoun Square; where it is located. The square is named after Thatcher Magoun, a Medford shipbuilding magnate in the mid 19th century.

Orleans

65 Holland Street   617.591.2100

open daily 11am 'til 1am

Orleans has a sophistication you don't often find in a neighborhood bar. With comfortable couches, low tables, French windows and a great patio; Orleans is a perfect place to relax with friends and enjoy a drink or a meal. Their cuisine has garnered rave reviews from many local critics. Extensive draught selection, wine menu and drinks list.

Food: The menu at Orleans offers a wide variety of interesting choices. Favorites include Chicken Spezzatino, Spice Rubbed Salmon Filet and Baby Arugula Pizza. Belgian Beer and Mussels served Tuesday nights.

Entertainment: DJs Wednesday and Thursday. Bands on Friday and Saturday. All sports are available on their 5 TVs; including the NFL and MLB packages.

What's In A Name: The pub is named after the town of Orleans on Cape Cod.

P.J. Ryan's

239 Holland St.   617.625.8200

open Mon - Thu 4pm 'til 1am,
Fri noon 'til 2am, Sat 10:30am 'til 2am,
Sun 10:30am 'til 1am

Very popular with the young Somerville and Tufts University crowds. A great diversion from the Davis Square scene, which is only a ten-minute walk away.

Food: P.J. Ryan's serves a great Irish-American pub food menu of burgers, sandwiches, salads and tasty appetizers. The Black & Blue Burger is excellent. Breakfast choices, including great omelets and a full Irish Breakfast are served on weekends.

Entertainment: Live bands performing all types of music play Wednesday, Thursday and Saturday nights. DJ on Fridays. Pub Quiz is played Tuesdays at 9:30pm. Traditional Seisiun Sundays at 6pm. All the games: rugby, soccer, NFL, NBA, NHL, baseball and more are shown at P.J. Ryan's.

What's In A Name: There's nothing to the name other than the owners liking it.

R.F. O'Sullivan & Son

282 Beacon Street   617.492.7773

open daily 11am 'til 1am

Its no-nonsense, hospitable approach has produced a legion of loyal patrons at R.F. O'Sullivan & Son. The clientele is a mix from the neighborhood and the local universities. Often someone will become a familiar face while going to school nearby and after graduation realize that they can't get enough of O'Sullivan's; so they return for a bite, a pint and a chat.

Food: Lots of places boast of serving the "best burger in town" but we're telling you, hands down; this is the place. They don't muck about at O'Sullivan's where all the burgers are made from a half-pound of ground sirloin and served with Sullie's Fries. A different specialty burger is featured each night. They also have a pretty good selection of entrees including veggie options and do a great London Fish & Chips.

Entertainment: The jukebox, TV and whoever is sitting next to you.

What's In A Name: R.F. O'Sullivan & Son is named after its owner and, of course, his son.

Sally O'Brien's

335 Somerville Avenue   617.666.3589

open daily 11am 'til 1am

Sally O'Brien's is a hopping Union Square spot that's popular with locals stopping in for a bite at lunchtime and music lovers coming to see the bands.

Food: The food at Sally O'Brien's is standard pub fare with plenty of options and it's quite good. Outstanding burgers. A brunch is served on Sunday.

Entertainment: Comedy followed by Karaoke on Mondays. Live bands Tuesday and Thursday through Sunday. Wednesday is Poker night with prizes. Sally's has two 42" plasma TVs for watching the games, including all the top international matches. They also have a jukebox along with Golden Tee Golf and other video games.

What's In A Name: Sally O'Brien was a beautiful and popular Irish model who was the star of the campaign which launched Harp Beer. The famous line from the campaign was "Sally O'Brien and the way she might look at you."

Sligo Pub

237A Elm Street   617.623.9651

open daily 8am 'til 1am

The license for the Sligo Pub has been at the same address since prohibition. Its a small, one room "dive with character." The back half of the room is covered in the graffiti of patrons leaving their mark over the years. The Sligo is popular among students and young professionals along with many long time local patrons.

Food: No kitchen. Bar snacks are available.

Entertainment: Cool jukebox and a TV.

What's In A Name: Named after County Sligo in northwest Ireland.

Thirsty Scholar

70 Beacon Street   617.497.2294

open daily 11am 'til 1am

The Thirsty Scholar is the place where you'll always find good food, good beer and good company. One of the nicer pubs in the Boston area and its owners are two of the city's nicest guys. The Thirsty Scholar was featured on Racheal Ray's Tasty Travels.

Food: The Thirsty Scholar serves up traditional pub fare and Irish favorites of impeccable quality. Everything on the menu is under $14. There are specials available each day for lunch and dinner. On Sundays a magnificent brunch is served 'til 2pm.

Entertainment: Trivia on Sundays. The Thirsty Scholar hosts poetry readings and book signings. A big screen TV shows broadcasts of sporting events and there's always cool music wafting in the background.

What's In A Name: The pub was given its name due to its proximity to Harvard University and the legions of "thirsty scholars" who find it a welcome respite from the many hours spent in study.

The Spirit of The Nog Lives On!

For those of you heartbroken over the closing of Union Square institution Tír na nÓg (that would be all of us), we're happy to let you all know that Robert and Ronan are keeping the spirit alive just down the street at Toast Lounge where they're booking the music for "nÓg Nights."

Toast Lounge
70 Union Square,
Somerville
617.623.9211
www.ToastLounge.com

JAMAICA PLAIN, MISSION HILL

Brendan Behan

378 Centre Street   617.522.5386

open daily Noon 'til 1am

The patrons are the main focus at The Brendan Behan as there are no pinball or video games to distract from the lively conversation among the devoted regulars. Ireland's Sunday Tribune has called The Behan "Boston's best watering hole."

Food: No kitchen. Bar snacks are available and you can get delivery from local restaurants.

Entertainment: Irish bands on Saturdays from 4pm 'til 7pm. Pub Quiz on Tuesdays. There's a dart board and darts are very popular at The Behan. TVs for watching the matches.

What's In A Name: Brendan Francis Behan (1923 - 1964) was an Irish poet, short story writer, novelist and playwright who wrote in both Irish and English. He was also a committed Irish Republican and an erstwhile member of the Irish Republican Army. Supposedly court-martialled from the IRA at an early age, he explained: "Yes, I was court-martialled in my absence, and sentenced to death in my absence. So I said 'go ahead and shoot me...in my absence!'"

Doyle's

3484 Washington Street
617.524.2345

open daily 9am 'til 1am

Doyle's has been a Jamaica Plain and Boston institution for well over a century. The past, present and future of Boston politics have all enjoyed cold beers along with heated debates at Doyle's. It's a place where you can eat well, rich or poor. There are over fifty beers available, ranging from $2.25 drafts to $7 bottles. Finton Coogan, the mayor of Galway, called Doyle's "the best pub outside of County Galway." National Geographic Magazine referred to Doyle's as "a hallowed Hibernian bar." But perhaps legendary Boston mayor Kevin White said it best: "I was born in JP, baptized at Saint Thomas Church and hung out at Doyle's. What else could a man ask from life!"

Food: The kitchen is open daily 'til 11pm. They have all the pub favorites: burgers, sandwiches, pizzas along with a selection of generous entrees. There's always a few fresh fish selections. The Prime Rib, New Zealand Baby Lamb Chops and Alaskan Salmon are all very popular. Brunch is served Saturday and Sunday 'til 3pm.

Entertainment: Aside from the TVs the entertainment is you, your mates and those you meet.

What's In A Name: The pub was originally owned by the Doyle brothers, who owned a lot of property in the neighborhood and opened Doyle's in 1882.

Flann O'Brien's

1619 Tremont Street   617.566.7744

open daily 10am 'til 1:30am

Flann's is a small, traditional Irish pub with a great staff and young, attractive customers. It has a nice, cozy interior and one of the best exteriors you'll find on any Irish pub. Flann's is wicked fun on weekends.

Food: Served daily 'til 10pm, Brunch on Sunday. Menu includes wraps, sandwiches, home soups and beef stew, fish & chips, shepherd's pie and burgers. There are daily $5 lunch and dinner specials. Full menu at www.flanns.com

Entertainment: Trivia on Tuesdays, DJ on Thursdays and Karaoke on Saturdays. Pool table, jukebox, local sports on the big screen TV.

What's In A Name: "Flann O'Brien" was the *nom de plume* of Irish novelist and satirist Brian O'Nolan (1911 - 1966), a major figure in 20th century Irish literature best known for his novels An Béal Bocht, At Swim-Two-Birds and The Third Policeman.

James's Gate

5-11 McBride Street · 617-983-2000

open Mon 4pm 'til 1am,
Tue - Sat 11:30am 'til 1am,
Sun Noon 'til 1am

James's Gate is a popular, traditional pub which plays host to a diverse collection of Jamaica Plain regulars. Rotating original art is featured on its walls. There's a wonderful fireplace to cozy up to during the winter. The facade is a replica of Guinness' Saint James's Gate Brewery in Dublin. Winner of a Best Of Boston award from Boston Magazine in 2005. A great place to rally with friends and family; true Irish pub fraternity.

Food: The kitchen is closed on Mondays. The traditional pub lunch menu features Fish & Chips, Sausages, Bangers & Mash with mushy peas, Chips & Curry, burgers, etc. The restaurant dinner menu includes steaks, seafood and pastas and has been described by the Boston Globe as "hearty meets high-end." Brunch offered on Sundays. Daily specials.

Entertainment: Pub Quiz on Monday nights. American and foreign sporting events are shown on the big screen TVs. Art openings.

What's In A Name: Leased for 9,000 years in 1759 by Arthur Guinness at £45 per year, Saint James's Gate Brewery in Dublin is the home of Guinness. It is named for Saint James's Gate, located off the south quays of Dublin, on James Street, which was the western entrance to the city during the middle ages.

Curley Mansion

Mayor James Michael Curley had this twenty-one room Georgian Revival mansion built in 1915 by contractor Thomas O'Connor. The shamrocks carved into the 30 window shutters served as a symbol of the emergence of the Irish in Boston politics. Located at 350 Jamaicaway, in Jamaica Plain, the mansion is now owned by the City of Boston.

Jeannie Johnston

144 South Street   617.983.9432

open Mon - Thurs 3pm 'til 1am,
Fri & Sat noon 'til 2am, Sun noon 'til 1am

The Jeannie Johnston sports an easy-going ambiance, hands-on ownership, a friendly staff, and cool regulars; which make this pub a great local hang. They attract a diverse crowd and everyone is welcome at this well-rounded pub.

Food: The menu features a good selection of American pub fare; burgers, ribs, pastas, etc. Nothing on the menu is priced more than $12. Specials are available daily.

Entertainment: Trivia on Wednesdays. Events with prizes on Thursdays. Live bands on Saturdays. Karaoke on Saturdays (total crazy fun). They have Golden Tee Golf and big screen TVs for watching the games. 25¢ wings during Monday Night Football.

What's In A Name: Of all Ireland's emigrant vessels, the Jeannie Johnston (1847-1858) was the most famous and had the proudest record. On her sixteen voyages, to Baltimore, New York and Quebec between 1848 and 1855 she lost not a single passenger.

J.J. Foley's Fireside Tavern

30 Hyde Park Avenue   no phone

open daily 10am 'til 2am

The Fireside Tavern is one large open room featuring a huge horseshoe bar and old-school stools and tables along the walls. Entering this pub is like stepping into a time capsule from the 1950's. It seems like Foley's knew if they waited long enough, the "regular guy style" decor would be back in fashion. The staff is amusing and affable with spot-on bartending. Cheers to the colorful cast of regulars who hang here. (They should create a television sitcom with these guys in mind!) They'll welcome you with friendly wise-cracking conversation; creating an unforced fun atmosphere. A must visit for any true Boston pub groupie.

Food: Hot dogs, chips and pretzels.

Entertainment: Juke Box, 2 dart boards, 3 TVs and a large screen, pinball, video game, and 2 chess and checker boards...plus the banter at the bar.

What's In A Name: The pub is named after John Joseph Foley who emigrated to America from Kerry in 1909. Oh, and there's a fireplace.

Penguin

735 Huntington Ave.   617.277.9200

open Mon - Fri 11am 'til 1am,
Sat & Sun noon 'til 1am

Clean and comfortable; relax with a beer and pizza or take it home. This healthy treat is available in white and whole wheat pizza dough. The sauces are sugar free and made with all natural ingredients. They do their best to avoid saturated and trans fats. This pizza pad isn't exactly an "Irish Pub" but they do have a new expanded bar, honest Irish ownership and management, Irish quality and of course they serve Guinness. Healthy pizza, wonderful management and tons of fun make it easy to remember their slogan, "Eat here and live, love and laugh longer.

Food: Original gourmet thin-crust pizzas made with fresh dough at plain old pizza prices. Try the Duck Confit Pizza; slow cooked duck, roasted potato, roasted red onion and fontina. Or the Smoked Salmon Pizza: Smoked salmon, kalamata olives, red onion, scallion and lemon fraiche. They also have a nice selection of pasta dishes, Panini Tostadas and wraps.

Entertainment: Juke box for tunes and flat screens for the news and sports.

What's In A Name: A penguin makes for a well-dressed formal logo. Penguin Fun Fact: Penguins are only native to the Southern Hemisphere. They can be found in Antarctica, the South American coast, South Africa, The Galapagos, southern Australia and New Zealand. We bet they'd love Shrimp Pizza.

Squealing Pig

134 Smith Street   617.566.6651

open Sun - Wed 11am 'til midnight,
Thu - Sat 11am 'til 2am

The Squealing Pig has a diverse and loyal clientele which is reflective of its neighborhood. During the day it's very popular with the doctors, nurses and hospital crowd from nearby Longwood Medical Area. At night you'll find a mix of locals from Mission Hill and Jamaica Plain along with students from Harvard Medical School and Northeastern University.

Food: "The Pig" offers the usual assortment of pub grub, and they do it quite well. They serve a great quesadilla, the best of which may be the Peking Duck. The star attraction of the Squealing Pig's menu is their 'Toasties', or grilled sandwiches. Some favorites are the Cubano, the Grilled Bacon & Cheese and the Turkey Reuben. Toasties are served 'til midnight.

Entertainment: Live bands entertain on Saturday nights. International sporting matches on the projection TV.

What's In A Name: One of the pub's owners grew up in Derry, where there was a pub named the Squealing Pig. She always liked the name.

SOUTH BOSTON

Aces High

551 Dorchester Avenue   617.269.7637

open daily 8am 'til 1am

Established in 1972 and filled with nostalgic charm; they've got it all at Aces High, which is a game room morphed into a pub. Nice smoking patio out back. "Put yourself in our place," says proprietor Jimmy Brennan.

Food: The food at Aces High consists of pizzas and club sandwiches.

Entertainment: There are 8 TVs, a jukebox, pool tables, dart boards, Golden Tee Golf and other video games. They've even got horseshoes out back. Full service lottery.

What's In A Name: The owner, Jimmy Brennan, named his pub after his father, who was quite a baseball pitcher in his day and was known as "Ace" Brennan.

Blackthorn Bar

471 West Broadway   617.269.5510

open Mon - Sat 10am 'til 1am,
Sun noon 'til 1am

Opened in 1990 as South Boston's first native Irish owned bar, The Blackthorn is a traditional Victorian era pub offering a true Irish environment with no phony props or people. It is well known among the young Irish immigrants in our city.

Food: No food. Bar snacks available.

Entertainment: Live bands and DJs on weekends. Three plasma TVs showing all the GAA, Irish football and international soccer. They have darts, a pool table and a great jukebox.

What's In A Name: Stems from the blackthorn, a small fruit tree, have traditionally been used for making shillelaghs.

Boston Beer Garden

732 East Broadway   617.269.0990

open Mon - Fri 11:30am 'til 1am,
Sat & Sun 10am 'til 1am

The Boston Beer Garden is known for its laid back, relaxed atmosphere. A wonderful pub for casual dining. They aim to please. In fact, if you don't find anything on the menu you want they'll take your request. Improper Bostonian Magazine named Boston Beer Garden "Best Neighborhood Bar."

Food: Served daily 'til 11pm. The Boston Beer Garden is famous around town for its fresh pasta dishes, great sandwiches and overall menu selection. Brunch is served Saturday and Sunday 'til 3pm and is the best hangover cure in the city.

Entertainment: No live music, but a sound system with one of the biggest and best playlists you'll find anywhere. The music choices are made up daily and are never stale. If there is any sporting event on in the world, you can bet it'll be on at the Beer Garden. NFL Sunday Ticket. Free WiFi internet access.

What's In A Name: With almost 40 beers available, this is Boston's beer garden.

The Clock

342 West Broadway   617.269.2480

open Mon - Sat 8am 'til Midnight,
Sun Noon 'til Midnight

The Clock Tavern has an old fashioned, no frills saloon feel. Antique Southie photos and prints hang on the walls. Plenty of clocks decorate the room so you'll never miss last call. Bartending is a serious business here, they are expert pint builders and clever at creating cocktails; the authentic Irish clientele would have it no other way. Late afternoons and early evenings the pub is filled with hard working craftsmen relaxing after an honest day's work. Later at night and on the weekends the clientele is more white collar. Worn, but not shabby the Clock Tavern is a endearing no pressure pub.

Food: No kitchen.

Entertainment: Pool table and darts. Two flat screen plasma TVs for all the games. They have a good jukebox and the MA Lottery's KENO game.

What's In A Name: The pub is named for the giant E. Howard Co. landmark clock located out front.

Dorchester Heights Monument

Local Irish colonists played a significant role in the Battle Of Dorchester Heights, which culminated in the evacuation of Boston by the British on March 17, 1776.

The password among the patriots that day was "Boston." The reply password was "Saint Patrick."

The Dorchester Heights Monument is located behind South Boston High School, which is on G Street.

Farragut House

149 P Street   617.268.6348

open daily 11am 'til 1am

Just up the road from Pleasant Bay the newly renovated Farragut House offers the perfect seaside pub setting, an ideal spot for drinks and dining before or after a Castle Island stroll. Comfortable classic pub furnishings, Farragut House is cozy and neat. A reflection on its location, there is a touch of a nautical motif. The walls are filled with Irish artifacts, Gaelic themed posters, Irish memorabilia and photos of Irish heroes from South Boston and beyond. The ownership is extremely experienced; the staff is well trained and aims to please. The Farragut House offers fantastic food, a supreme location and exemplary pub ambience.

Food: Lunch, Dinner and Sunday Brunch. They serve all your favorite Irish and American dishes but specialize in fresh fish. No less than twelve seafood dishes are on the menu, plus wonderful Catch Of The Day entrees. Fantastic lobster specials!

Entertainment: Live Music, occasionally a DJ or special entertainment. Monday is Traditional Irish Music, Thursday features the Blues, Friday is Karaoke night, and Irish Folk on Saturdays.

What's In A Name: The pub is named for Civil War hero Admiral David Farragut, famous for his quote at the Battle of Mobile Bay, "Damn the torpedoes, full speed ahead!" Anyone who has driven down East Broadway through Southie to Castle Island has noticed the Statue of Admiral Farragut overlooking Marine Park.

The Junction

110 Dorchester Street   617.268.6429

open daily 11am 'til 1am

The Junction is a great party spot. It's a huge pub with a remodeled interior done in traditional fashion. The food is quite good here; and sports fans find it to be one of the best venues in the city for watching a game.

Food: The Junction is famous throughout Southie for its hearty food and generous portions. The menu runs from Fish & Chips to Lobster and covers a lot of ground in between.

Entertainment: Trivia on Tuesdays. Live bands and DJs entertain Wednesday through Saturday. All GAA games, rugby, european soccer and american sporting events are shown on the TVs.

What's In A Name: The pub is located near the busy "junction" of Broadway and Dorchester Street.

Kelly's Landing

81 L Street   617.268.8900

open daily 11:30am 'til 1am

Kelly's Landing is a nice family-style restaurant with an excellent, friendly staff. In Southie this truly is the spot "where old friends meet."

Food: Best known for its fresh seafood offerings, such as lobster, Fried Clams and award-winning Clam Chowder; Kelly's Landing also serves up great steaks, chops and poultry along with burgers and sandwiches.

Entertainment: TVs and lottery.

What's In A Name: The original Kelly's Landing was opened by Larry and Ma Kelley in 1927 on South Boston's City Point shoreline. A mention of the original Kelly's to Southie old-timers will evoke a flow of old memories of walking the South Boston Strandway on a date with a "French Fry" and topping off the evening with an ice cream cone. The original location is etched in history and memorialized by the continued Kelly's tradition. The name is also landmarked on Coast Guard maps as an official site.

L Street Tavern

195 L Street   617.268.4335

open Sun - Thu noon 'til 1am, Fri & Sat 8am 'til 1am

The L Street Tavern is best known to outsiders from the film "Good Will Hunting," but has been a favorite among locals going back long before that. Renovated since the movie, but with all of its charm intact. This place gets packed on weekends.

Food: No kitchen; but feel free to bring your own.

Entertainment: 5 flat-screen TVs, jukebox, video games.

What's In A Name: We have a hunch the pub's name might have something to do with its address.

Murphy's Law

837 Summer Street   617.269.6667

open daily 10am 'til 2am

Located mid-way between South Station and South Boston's busy Broadway, Murphy's Law is a cool pub with great bartenders, interesting regulars and fantastic beer prices. Parts of Ben Affleck's movie Gone, Baby, Gone were filmed here.

Food: No kitchen, but pizza is available at the bar.

Entertainment: Open Mic on Thursdays. There are TVs, 2 dart boards and a jukebox.

What's In A Name: Murphy's Law ("Anything that can co wrong, will go wrong.") was conceived in 1949 at Edwards Air Force Base and is named after Capt. Edward A. Murphy, an engineer who was working on a project. One day, after finding that a transducer was wired wrong, he cursed the technician responsible saying "If there's any way to do it wrong; he'll find it." The project leader kept a list of "laws" and added this one, which he dubbed "Murphy's Law."

The Playwright

658 East Broadway   617.269.2537

open Mon - Fri 11:30am 'til 1am,
Sat & Sun 10:30am 'til 1am

The Playwright's handsome, stylish interior matches its patrons. This youthful, well manicured crowd isn't afraid to cut loose on weekends. Named "Neighborhood Bar Of The Year" by Improper Bostonian in 2004.

Food: The Playwright serves contemporary American cuisine with a wide variety of pastas and salad plates. Lunch and dinner specials are offered daily. The Homestyle Meatloaf is very tasty. A great brunch is served Saturdays and Sundays 'til 3pm.

Entertainment: Trivia on Thursdays. The Playwright has a computerized sound system playing top 40 and dance music nightly. The play list, which includes over 500 songs, is updated monthly. Eight TVs, including two big screens, feature satellite broadcasts of American and international sports.

What's In A Name: Well, the Irish are a literary people, and The Playwright is on Broadway...

Shannon Tavern

558 East 3rd Street
617.269.9460

open Mon - Sat 9am 'til 1am, Sun noon 'til 1am

The truly authentic old-school neighborhood tavern may be a vanishing breed, but it's living on strong and proud at The Shannon. This is one of our favorite new additions to this book. You enter a long barroom dripping with the type of charm that can't be laid on by a designer, only earned through years of service to your patrons. The barroom gives way to a game room behind the bar that's more in the style of the funnest "rec room" you'll find. Beers and food are good and cheap. Added to that; owner/bartender Jerry is a terrific guy.

Food: The Shannon's menu is a sampling of good barroom grub. They make awesome burgers, plus pizzas, deli sandwiches, shaved steak and the like. The Pastrami Sandwich is exceptional and there's usually a few special items for the day.

Entertainment: Karaoke a couple times a month. Pool, darts, Bubble Hockey, Golden Tee, internet jukebox with over 20,000 songs, plenty of TVs including a big projection screen.

What's In A Name: The pub was opened in 1960 by current owner Jerry Bowen's dad, who came over from Ireland by boat in 1948. Jerry's mom came over in 1952, but by plane. Flying out of Shannon Airport instead of Dublin, her plane was struck by lightning and lost a propeller as it neared America, but was able to land safely. They'd often mused that if the plane was coming from Dublin and had that extra 140 miles to go, it may not have made it. So the choice of Shannon Airport was deemed lucky and fortuitous.

Shenannigans

332 West Broadway   617.269.9509

open daily 11am 'til 1am

Shenannigans is a sharp looking Southie haunt with fine cuisine and a cool vibe. Great place to hang out in the summer; when the french windows are thrown open.

Food: Shenannigan's menu consists of Irish, international and sauteed dishes. There's always a few daily specials. A breakfast menu is served Sundays 'til 3pm.

Entertainment: Karaoke on Thursdays. A mix of bands and DJs Wednesday, Friday and Saturday. DJ on Sunday. International soccer, rugby and hurling matches are shown on the TVs.

What's In A Name: Shenannigans are high-spirited or mischievous antics.

Tom English's Cottage

112 Emerson Street
617.269.9805

open daily 8am 'til 1am

Tom English's Cottage is a friendly, neighborhood pub with a casual atmosphere and great prices. Very popular place to watch the game on the tube and shoot some stick.

Food: A basic but good pub grub menu is served Tuesday through Sunday noon 'til 8pm.

Entertainment: Darts, pool, jukebox and video games.

What's In A Name: The pub is named after its owner, Tom English.

PubCorner.com

DORCHESTER ▶

The Banshee

934 Dorchester Avenue   617.436.9747

open daily 10am 'til 1am

Whatever you're looking for; whatever your idea of a good time is, you'll find it at The Banshee. They've got a great staff and an interesting crowd of patrons from all backgrounds and professions. Everyone mingles well. Nice room upstairs available for private functions.

Food: The kitchen is open 'til 10pm Monday through Saturday and 7pm on Sundays. The cuisine is mostly Irish-American offering a selection of grilled dinners, pastas, soups and salads. The 15oz. Shepherd's Pie is fantastic! A great Irish breakfast is served all day, every day and is the "star" of The Banshee's Sunday Brunch. Two specials are offered each day.

Entertainment: The Banshee has it all. They show all international sporting events. Entertainment ranging from DJs and live bands to traditional seisiún performs Thursday through Monday nights. Pool and darts are available. The second floor offers an oasis away from the crowd at night.

What's In A Name: Loosely translated Banshee means ghost. The Banshee is a beautiful woman with long, flowing red hair who comes to you singing and wailing. When she does come; someone close to you is going to die.

The Bar

1221 Dorchester Avenue
617.288.5900

open daily noon 'til 1am

Nondescript on the outside, but pub-pretty on the inside, The Bar is a favorite meeting place for people from the neighborhood and is very popular among the extended local Irish community.

Food: No kitchen.

Entertainment: TVs for watching the games, a pool table, jukebox, video games and internet access.

What's In A Name: Sometimes it's tough to come up with a name, so the owners decided to simply call this place what it is.

Blarney Stone

1505 Dorchester Avenue
617.436.8223

open daily 11am 'til 1am

Blarney Stone leads the way in design for modern Irish bars with its hip interior. It boasts a top-range sound system. For years Blarney Stone has been a first stop for newly arrived immigrants and visitors arriving in Boston.

Food: The Blarney Stone's menu includes a great selection of sandwiches, wraps and salads for lunch. Dinner items from New York Sirloin to pastas to Fish & Chips. Brunch is served on Sunday.

Entertainment: A DJ entertains Wednesday through Saturday. 2 pool tables. International soccer and rugby matches and NFL Sunday Ticket™ are shown on several TVs including a 10 ft. projection screen.

What's In A Name: The Blarney Stone is a block of bluestone built into the battlements of Blarney Castle, about 5 miles north of Cork. According to legend, kissing the stone endows the kisser with the gift of gab.

Centre Bar

1664 Dorchester Avenue
617.436.0707

open daily 11am 'til 1am

Formerly Desmonds, the new Centre Bar is a fantastic pub done out in traditional style. It's fast becoming a favorite among Dorchester's many Irish. It's a nice, big open room with a long bar and plenty of room for mingling. A stone fireplace keeps things toasty in winter. Their terrific staff is just one of the reasons you'll find yourself coming back again and again.

Food: Centre Bar serves food on weekends. The menu includes a nice selection of hearty traditional favorites, including Irish Breakfast. They make the best Chicken Curry in Dorchester.

Entertainment: Live bands Saturday and every other Sunday. All the international sporting matches on the plasma TVs. Dart board and jukebox.

What's In A Name: The pub is located at the corner of Dorchester Avenue and Centre Street.

C.F. Donovan's

112 Savin Hill Ave.   617.436.2226

open Mon - Sat 11am 'til 1am,
Sun noon 'til 1am

A capitol pub for a jovial chat. Appreciable serving sizes, exquisite meals. Hands on ownership that really cares for its customers. A warm-hearted staff that caters to every need. A good pint, excellent company, great food and terrific service; C.F. Donovan's creates perfect pubbing.

Food: Unique, fresh and scrumptious. Lunch menu features salads (Crispy Scallop Salad), sandwiches (Lobster Club), entrees (Parmesan Crusted Haddock), omelets (Florentine Cheese Omelet). Dinner menu offers steaks (Filet Mignon), chicken dishes (Chicken Curry), seafood (Lobster Pie, Scallops, Whole Clams) and pasta (Linguine Del Mare, Penne Con Polo, Penne Alla Buttera).

Entertainment: Trivia on Tuesdays. DJs on the weekends. All the important games on their 4 big flat screens plus a projection TV.

What's In A Name: The owner named his pub in honor of his father.

Eire Pub

795 Adams Street   617.436.0088

**open Mon - Sat 8am 'til Midnight,
Sun noon 'til Midnight**

The Eire is a pub with a wonderful, neighborhood feel to it, packed with interesting patrons engaged in lively conversation.   The pub was made famous on January 26, 1983 when, during a visit to Boston, President Ronald Reagan stopped by the Eire for a Ballantine Ale.

Food: Hearty pub grub, with a great selection of generous sandwiches. The Eire does a great lunch trade.

Entertainment: The Eire Pub is very popular with the local sports fans and they have 11 TVs.

What's In A Name: "Eire Pub" is gaelic for Irish pub.

Gerard's

776 Adams Street   617.282.6370

open daily 6:30am 'til 1am

Gerard's is a cheery little restaurant/pub located directly next door to the historic Gerard's General Market. You must cut across the very busy market "speakeasy-style" to find the entrance to the restaurant. Pass through this door and into the quiet and relaxed vibe of the pub. The pub is divided into three regions; one space dedicated to the bar area and two other more intimate areas for dining. Not really a "drinking bar," they specialize in serving the freshest and highest quality cuisine in a quaint Victorian atmosphere. With great food and a caring staff a visit to Gerard's has become "tradition" in this close-knit Adam's Village community.

Food: Serving breakfast, lunch and dinner. Very extensive menus for all meals. Omelet station, waffles, Irish Breakfast. Irish specialties, a nice selection of fresh seafood dishes. The Chicken Alexander is fantastic.

Entertainment: TVs at the bar.

What's In A Name: The owner is Gerard Adomunes.

the Druid

What a true Irish Pub should be... ...a social experience.

Stop by The Druid where you'll find a unique yet low-key and relaxing atmosphere. Whether having a pint with your friends, dining on some of the best pub food in the city, or taking in one of our frequent events; you'll find the warmth of home at The Druid.

Kitchen open noon 'til 10pm Mon – Sat
Brunch on Sundays 10am 'til 4pm

Open Sun – Wed 11am 'til 1am; Thu – Sat 'til 2am
1357 Cambridge Street • Inman Sq., Cambridge
617.497.0965 • www.druidpub.com

Wednesdays
Boston's Best Pub Quiz
at 8pm

Thursdays
College Night with DJ
Nighttime Gallagher at 10pm

Fridays
Traditional Irish Seisiun
with Chris McGrath and
Noel Scott. 6 - 10pm.
All musicians welcome

Saturdays
DJ Ren Justice with
special guests at 9:30pm

NEVER A COVER CHARGE

First O'Neill's Pub
DUBLIN, 1890

Hugh O'Neill's

IRISH PUB & RESTAURANT

TUESDAY > GENERAL TRIVIA PUB QUIZ
WEDNESDAY > SPORTS & ENTERTAINMENT PUB QUIZ
THURSDAY through SATURDAY > DJs

SERVING LUNCH, DINNER & WEEKEND BRUNCH
AMERICAN CUISINE plus IRISH FAVORITES..."LEAGUES
BEYOND PUB GRUB."

READERS' CHOICE AWARD > BEST BAR IN
MALDEN: 2005, 2006...

RUGBY, ENGLISH PREMIER LEAGUE & EUROPEAN
SOCCER...EXTENSIVE BEER SELECTION...FREE WI-FI

45 Pleasant Street in Malden Center
781.338.9977
www.HughONeills.com

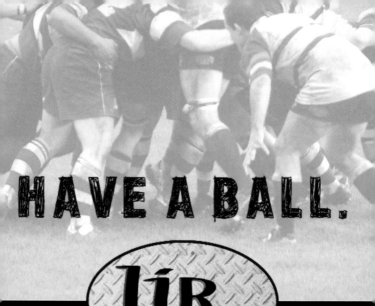

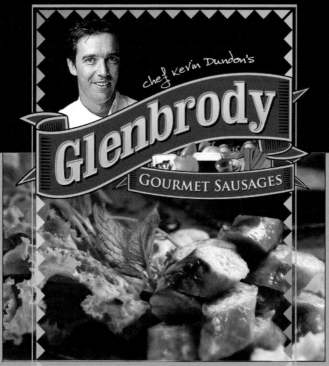

Tommy Moloney's

www.tommymoloneys.com
1-800-431-6365

chef Kevin Dundon's

Glenbrody

GOURMET SAUSAGES

WWW.GLENBRODY.COM

Proudly distributed in Boston by
Limerick Meats & Provisions   617-442-8844

And **SEXY PARTY SATURDAYS** with DJ Greg G

CATCH ALL THE GAMES
ON OUR 15 NEW FLAT
SCREEN TVs!

ENJOY $2 BEERS!

Kitty O'Sheas

131 STATE STREET, BOSTON
617.725.0100

BOSTON'S OLDEST, NEWEST HOT SPOT!

www.KittyOSheasBoston.com · www.MySpace.com/KittyOSheas

HONEY FITZ PUB

est. 1985

GET DOWN OFF THE COUCH...

...AND HEAD UP TO THE FITZ!!

PUB TRIVIA on Mondays. Prizes to be won and a good time for all...

...BAR PONG on Thursdays. Come join the fun. Cash prize to the winning team...

...KARAOKE on Wednesdays. Strut those vocal chords and break out the cheesy ballads...

...Plus BANDS, DJs, COMEDY NIGHTS, DARTS, POOL, BIG SCREEN TV, VIDEO GAMES, GREAT PUB GRUB, GOOD BEER SELECTION...

...Well, what are you waiting for?

142 Pleasant Street, Malden
one block from Malden Center Station
www.HoneyFitzPub.com
781.324.0111

The Harp & Bard

1099 Dorchester Avenue   617.265.2893

open daily 11am 'til 1am

The Harp & Bard is a very popular neighborhood pub and family style restaurant. They have a nice outdoor patio where you can catch some rays while having a bite and a pint during the summer. A function room is available for private parties and the catering service is terrific.

Food: The menu features American style cooking such as steaks, chops, chicken, fresh seafood and hearty soups which are made from scratch each day. Lunch is served 'til 4pm, dinner 'til 11pm. The Prime Rib might be the biggest in the city.

Entertainment: Trivia on Thursdays. The Harp & Bard is a great place to catch your favorite sporting events as there are 20 TVs. A DJ entertains on holidays.

What's In A Name: A Harp is a musical instrument and the national emblem of Ireland. A Bard is a celtic minstrel.

J.J.'s Irish Bar

1130 Dorchester Avenue
617.282.5919

open Mon - Sat 8am 'til 1am,
Sunday noon 'til 1am

J.J.'s is a comfortable local pub popular with the honest, hardworking neighborhood folk. No need to change after work; a come-as-you-are attitude works well here. J.J.'s is a terrific place to find an expert tradesman. On weekend nights the blue collar clientele turn out in their casual best to enjoy the good cheer at J.J.'s.

Food: J.J.'s serves up the usual pub sustenance including filling steak dinners and hearty sandwiches.

Entertainment: A competitive pool table, 4 TVs showing all the big games and a jukebox with a solid playlist.

What's In A Name: The two "J"s in J.J.'s Irish Bar are the first initials of the two original owners.

Nash's Pub

1154 Dorchester Avenue   617.436.4134

**open Mon - Sat 11am 'til 1am,
Sun Noon 'til 1am**

The good size back room and excellent sound system turn Nash's into a popular dance club on weekends. Nash's books talented bands and DJs that have a loyal following among the native Irish and local merry makers. The front maintains a more relaxed tone, allowing you to enjoy the games, your friends, and conversation.

Food: No kitchen. Bar snacks available.

Entertainment: Friday, Saturday and Sunday nights feature popular bands and DJs in the back room. In the front room you can catch all the soccer, rugby and Irish football matches, get in a dart game, or play some tunes on the jukebox.

What's In A Name: The pub is named after its owner, Peter Nash.

Peggy O'Neil's

1310 Dorchester Ave.   617.265.8846

**open Mon - Sat 10am 'til 2am,
Sun Noon 'til 2am**

Peggy O'Neil's is an institution along bustling Dorchester Avenue. There's something here for everyone, which attests to why you'll often find an interesting mix of folks at this lovely pub.

Food: Peggy O'Neil's serves lunch seven days a week from 11am 'til 2pm. The menu includes Steak Tips, Fish & Chips, Burgers, Lobster and Steaks. The Fries are homemade and are excellent.

Entertainment: Bands and DJs entertain on various nights. Peggy's has 6 TVs, a pool table, 3 dart boards, a jukebox, Golden Tee Golf and other video games.

What's In A Name: The owners named their pub after their beloved mother.

Tom English's

957 Dorchester Ave.
617.288.7748

open daily 8am 'til 1am

Tom English's is an old-school Dorchester watering hole. It's back to the basics here; a single rectangular room with a bar cutting through the middle. The Irish Breakfast here is quite good and a terrific value.

Food: Tom English's serves a typical pub menu of burgers and sandwiches. Irish Breakfast is served every day.

Entertainment: TVs, a dart board and a jukebox.

What's In A Name: The pub is named after its owner.

Twelve Bens

315 Adams Street   617.265.6727

open Mon - Sat 8am 'til 1am,
Sun noon 'til 1am

An authentic Boston neighborhood hangout. You'll mingle with "real" Bostonians and get an inside opinion on Boston politics and sports. Better know your facts and you better be rooting for the Sox and Pats. Good food, lots of sociable regulars and minimal prices.

Food: Your favorite pub grub plus grand steaks, delicious homemade Chicken Parmesan and pasta dishes, fantastic beef stew and more.

Entertainment: Darts, jukebox, and a slew of TVs covering all angles so you'll never miss a minute of the game.

What's In A Name: The Twelve Bens is a mountain range in Connemara in the west of Ireland.

HYDE PARK, ROSLINDALE, WEST ROXBURY

Corrib Pub

2030 Centre Street, West Roxbury
617.469.4177

open daily 11am 'til 2am

The West Roxbury Corrib, located on busy Centre Street, is equally popular with discriminating diners and nighttime revelers. This is the perfect place for a pint and a chat and to meet someone new.

Food: The kitchen is open 'til 10pm each day. They serve the usual pub fare of soups, salads and sandwiches along with a wide-ranging selection of beef, chicken, pasta and seafood entrees. Their Scrod Dinner and 17 oz. T-Bone Steak are very popular. A great brunch is served Sundays.

Entertainment: The West Roxbury Corrib is popular with sports fans who find it a great place to enjoy the games on TV. They run a lot of promotions and specials on Monday nights during the NFL season. DJ on Thursdays.

What's In A Name: Like its sister pubs in Brighton and Brookline, the Corrib Pub is named after Lough Corrib, a lake in County Galway.

Dempsey's

1185 River Street, Hyde Park
617.364.0770

open Mon - Sat 8:30am 'til 11pm,
Sun noon 'til 11pm

Dempsey's has a brilliant, easy atmosphere and is a very welcoming place for all who visit. Great place for hanging out.

Food: No kitchen.

Entertainment: Darts, pool table, TVs and a jukebox. A sing-along is likely to break out at any time among the regular clientele and newcomers are welcomed as regulars.

What's In A Name: Dempsey's is named after its owners, Oliver and Mary Dempsey.

J.J. Brannelly's

4432 Washington St., Roslindale
617.323.6700

open daily 11am 'til 1am

J.J. Brannelly's is an extremely popular Roslindale pub. It's a big, open room with the bar in the middle and a cast of interesting and friendly merrymakers on all sides. The ownership takes pride in all aspects of the pub business and it shows. Talk to a Brannelly's patron and they'll equally sing the praises of its hearty food, good times, crackerjack staff, and overall craic.

Food: Brannelly's offers up a full menu of delicious pub grub for lunch and dinner. The seafood here is quite good and the Chicken Parmesan is a popular choice.

Entertainment: Trivia on Wednesdays. Karaoke on Fridays. There are TVs for watching the games and they may be adding darts soon.

What's In A Name: This is a family owned and operated pub and it's named after the current owner's dad.

Maggie Mae's

635 Hyde Park Avenue, Roslindale
617.325.1514

open daily 10am 'til 1am

Maggie Mae's has a very cheerful, hard-working clientele. A great place to go for a mid-day bite or an evening pint with your pals. They have a great reputation in the neighborhood for their food.

Food: Maggie Mae's serves a traditional Irish-American menu with Irish Breakfast available every day. Popular choices are the Chicken with Broccoli & Ziti and the steaks.

Entertainment: A DJ entertains Friday nights. A band is brought in on Sunday afternoons. There are 2 dart boards and Golden Tee Golf.

What's In A Name: The pub's owner calls his wife Margaret "Maggie Mae."

Master McGrath's

1154 River Street, Hyde Park
617.364.3662

open Mon - Sat 9am 'til 1am,
Sun noon 'til 1am

Master McGrath's is probably the liveliest pub in Boston's Hyde Park neighborhood. They have a reputation for an ultra-friendly and efficient staff which certainly contributes to the loyalty of the clientele.

Food: Master McGrath's serves up a tasty menu of pub grub and traditional favorites. Lunch specials are offered each day except Sunday. Irish Breakfast is served all day, every day.

Entertainment: A DJ entertains Thursday nights. Trivia Quiz is played on Tuesday nights. GAA matches are shown live and darts are available.

What's In A Name: Master McGrath (1866 - 1871) was a legendary racing greyhound in Ireland. A small, weak pup he went on to become the most celebrated and successful dog of his time. He became such a celebrity that his owner, Lord Lurgan, was requested to take him to be seen by Queen Victoria and the Royal Family.

West Roxbury Pub

1885 Centre Street, West Roxbury
617.469.2624

open Mon - Sat 8am 'til 1am,
Sunday Noon 'til 1am

The West Roxbury Pub is Boston Irish at its heart. As much a family dining establishment as it is a pub. Wonderful mural depicting the life and exploits of James Michael Curley on every wall.

Food: The food at the West Roxbury Pub is fresh, with generous portions and wallet-friendly prices. The Boston Scrod, Broiled Pork Chops and Chicken Marsala are excellent.

Entertainment: Karaoke on Friday nights. Live bands on Saturday nights. TVs at the bar for watching the games.

What's In A Name: We'll let you guess why it's called the West Roxbury Pub.......*You're right!*

PubCorner.com

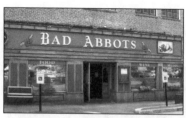

Bad Abbots

1546-Rear Hancock Street
617.774.1434

open daily 10am 'til 1am

You'll quickly get in the habit of Bad Abbots; a true Irish pub in decor and charm with the most authentic Irish ambiance. A wonderful spot to relax, practice the art of good conversation and enjoy great music. The barstaff will make you feel at home. You'll mingle easily in the regular guy and gal, good time crowd; a fun mix of local native Irish and others from the area.

Food: The finest pub fare featuring burgers, sandwiches and wraps, salads, and chicken, steak and seafood entrees. Irish breakfast is served all day every day. The $12 all-you-can-eat Sunday Brunch starts at 10am (price at time of publication).

Entertainment: All sporting events including soccer and rugby matches are carried live on the multiple TVs. Live bands entertain Thursday through Sunday nights. A Pub Trivia Quiz is played every Wednesday night. They also host Open Mic nights, dart tournaments and much more. Home of the Bad Abbot's Irish Music Festival.

What's In A Name: The theme of the pub, shown through its artwork, is that of a bad abbot. In other words one who, while mischievous, is also virtuous.

Black Water Tavern

35 Washington Street
617.770.0144

Open daily 11am 'til 1:30am

Black Water is a wonderful pub located in downtown Quincy just across from the Thomas Crane Public Library. Black Water is tidy and comfortable, the perfect size for an Irish pub; not so large that you'll lose your companions but not so small that you'll ever feel cramped. The interior features conventional-contemporary Irish pub décor. Pocket friendly prices, hands on management, a professional staff and friendly patrons make Black Water a fantastic night out.

Food: Serving the best Irish and American cuisine for brunch, lunch and dinner. Catering available for all functions.

Entertainment: Karaoke on Thursdays, DJ on Fridays, live bands on Saturdays. Plenty of TVs (including two huge HD plasmas) covering all the local and international sports. Darts, jukebox, multi-game video machine.

What's In A Name: One of the owners is from the Blackwater Valley in southeast Ireland. The River Blackwater (An Abhainn Mhór), one of the world's greatest Salmon fishing destinations, flows through the valley.

Callahan's

296 Copeland St.   617.472.9688

open daily 10am 'til 1am

Callahan's is a charming and cozy neighborhood pub. Located in a former Quincy firehouse, it's small inside (about 20' x 20') and adorned with lots of historic Quincy and Boston sports photos.

Food: Basic but hearty pub grub with a few specials offered each day.

Entertainment: TVs for watching the games; jukebox, video game, KENO.

What's In A Name: Owner Ed McNulty has a sign on an inside wall reading "McNulty's Pub;" but when he took over Callahan's he just kept the name the same.

Cronin's Publick House

23 Des Moines Road   617.786.9804

open daily 10am 'til 1am

There's been a bar at this location for over 66 years. Denis and Margaret Cronin took over in 1990 with the idea of combining top quality food and drink with the best in Irish hospitality. They've succeeded. Cronin's is a gem.

Food: Great pub fare. Cronin's web address says it all: www.SteakTips.com

Entertainment: DJs on weekend nights. 7 TVs for watching the games; Golden Tee Golf; an awesome jukebox; and full lottery.

What's In A Name: The pub is named for its late founder, Sgt. Denis P. Cronin, who hailed from County Kerry.

Goal Post

226 Water St.reet
617.471.6306

open daily 10am 'til 1am

This is a sports bar with a splash of Irish pub. TVs cover every angle, you'll never miss a pitch or punt. A great place to grab a bite, watch the game and talk sports with patrons who really know their stuff. Plenty of parking available.

Food: The Goal Post serves some of the heartiest pub grub in the area for lunch and dinner. Sandwiches, burgers, great steak tips.

Entertainment: Dart tournaments. 5 plasma TVs to cover all the games. Mostly American sports but they do show some of the european sports. They play music but keep the volume low, all focus is on the game. Jukebox and KENO.

What's In A Name: Goal Post is simply a great name for an Irish sports pub. Other pubs in Ireland and across the USA have the same name and attitude.

The Half Door

1516 Hancock Street   617.472.8600

open Mon - Sat 11am 'til 1am,
Sun 10am 'til 1am

Located in the heart of Quincy Center, The Half Door is the nucleus of the city's vibrant pub scene. Modern-antique design with lots of rough-cut exposed wood finished in an old world manner. Very comfortable surroundings; they have two bars for relaxing, discreet nooks for privacy and plenty of pleasant dining space.

Food: The Half Door's menu is innovative pub cuisine. Unique burgers, wraps, salads and entrees. Breakfast is served on weekends.

Entertainment: Pub Trivia on Tuesday. DJ on Thursday and Friday. Live band or DJ on Saturday. They have a dart board and great sports coverage on the TVs.

What's In A Name: A "half door" is a common feature of Irish cottages. It's a door, usually the main entry, where the top and bottom are split and can be opened and closed separately.

The Holy Ground

1600 Hancock Street   617.773.4334

open daily 10am 'til 1am

The Holy Ground is one of the best pubs in Greater Boston. Decorated in nautical and religious themes; a pub where good food is enjoyed with a pint and lively entertainment.

Food: The Holy Ground's menu is standard pub fare with plenty of Irish favorites. The Lamb Stew, Shepherd's Pie and Bangers & Mash are excellent. They do a great Irish Breakfast.

Entertainment: Live music most nights ranging from Irish traditional to dance DJs. Monday is Blues Night Open Mic. Pub Quiz is played every Tuesday. The weekly dart league is also on Tuesdays.

What's In A Name: The Holy Ground is a traditional Irish folk song named after an area in the town of Cobh, County Cork, on the south coast of Ireland which is known locally as "The Holy Ground." The name is ironic because in the 19th century the Holy Ground served as the town's red-light district.

The Irish Pub

51 Billings Road   617.774.0222

**open Mon - Sat 8am 'til 1am,
Sun Noon 'til 1am**

The Irish Pub boasts of being Quincy's most historic and authentic Irish pub. It's become the area's new-old "hot-spot" with a fresh "quiet-cool" vibe. They specialize in laid-back fun.

Food: Kitchen open Monday through Friday 11am 'til 7pm. Sandwiches, burgers and Irish fare. Fantastic specials everyday.

Entertainment: DJs Friday and Saturday night. Live music on Sundays. Electronic trivia.

What's In A Name: Well, it ain't an Italian restaurant.

Malachy's

51 Granite Street   617.472.9198

**open Mon - Sat 11am 'til 1am,
Sun noon 'til 1am**

Malachy's is an enjoyable Quincy local with a cheerful, attentive staff and relaxing atmosphere. They have a fiercely loyal band of regulars who'll swear to you up and down that Malachy's is the essence of what a true pub should be.

Food: Malachy's offers a traditional pub menu featuring fantastic deli sandwiches.

Entertainment: Darts and a pool table. One of the best jukeboxes in the area. Live bands occasionally.

What's In A Name: The pub is named after an old, well respected Dorchester barman named Malachy Higgins who emigrated from Tuam in County Galway.

Murphy's Twin Shamrocks

425 Hancock St.   617.770.9953

open Mon - Sat 10am 'til 1am,
Sun Noon 'til 1am

Murphy's Twin Shamrocks is a family owned and operated establishment which is equally appreciated as a friendly pub and for its excellent cuisine. You'll always find courteous service and great prices at Murphy's.

Food: Murphy's serves a fine menu of classic tavern fare along with a few Irish dishes. There are always a few specials on offer. Corned Beef is featured on Thursdays.

Entertainment: Pub Quiz on Wednesday. DJ Thursday through Saturday. Sporting events are shown on the TVs and darts are available.

What's In A Name: The pub is owned by the Murphy twins, David and Peter.

Paddy Barry's

1574 Hancock St.   617.770.3620

open daily 4pm 'til 1am

Paddy Barry's is a very popular, small pub in Quincy Center. The walls are covered with artifacts relating to both Irish and American traditions; a great mix of the old world and the new. The intimate setting makes Paddy Barry's one of the more enjoyable music venues in the area.

Food: No kitchen. Bar snacks available.

Entertainment: Paddy Barry's offers live traditional Irish, folk and other types of music Thursday through Sunday. Tuesday is Darts Night.

What's In A Name: The pub is named after an old Cork City pub named Paddy Barry's, which was a very popular sports pub.

Sarsfield's

1464 Hancock St.   617.773.2314

open Mon - Sat 8am 'til 1am,
Sun noon 'til 1am

Sarsfield's is a fine, traditional Irish pub and restaurant in the heart of Quincy Center. They pride themselves on high quality meals at very reasonable prices. The evenings are lively at Sarsfield's with top-notch entertainment. They boast of the best poured Guinness on Boston's South Shore.

Food: Sarsfield's menu is a mixture of Irish and American cuisine. Some favorites are the Irish Stew, Shepherd's Pie and Buffalo Style Chicken. A traditional Irish Breakfast is served every day. Terrific Brunch & Carvery (different style roast each week) served on Sundays.

Entertainment: DJs Friday, Saturday and Sunday. Sarsfield's is a favorite with the soccer, hurling, rugby and gaelic games crowd. Occasional live bands.

What's In A Name: The pub is named after Irish patriot Patrick Sarsfield who led the second flight of the Wild Geese. After the Treaty of Limerick, he marched to Cork with 11,000 soldiers and embarked for France. He died in the Battle of Landen in 1693.

Sly Fox

139 Copeland St.   617.328.5777

open Mon - Sat 11am 'til 1am,
Sun noon 'til 1am

The Sly Fox is a quaint place with a trendy decor. The atmosphere is very relaxed and gives the impression that this relative newcomer has been a neighborhood institution for years.

Food: The Sly Fox serves up traditional favorites like Irish Chicken Curry and Beef Stew along with quality pub staples like burgers, sandwiches and soups. The Roast Pork Tenderloin is incredible; it melts in your mouth. Bacon & Cabbage Dinner served Thursdays. The desserts at the Sly Fox are top-notch too. Save room for a piece of Carrot Cake or Sherry Trifle.

Entertainment: Traditional Irish bands entertain on Saturday or Sunday night. There's a jukebox, darts, 2 plasma TVs and KENO.

What's In A Name: The pub was named by owner Mary McKenna and her two daughters. There was a fox they used to see in their yard who they nicknamed the "Sly Fox."

NORTH OF BOSTON

The Blue Shamrock

105 Market Street, Lowell
978.458.1288

open daily 11am 'til 2am

There's two floors of fun at the Blue Shamrock, located in bustling downtown Lowell. It gets busy here on weekends, with lots of UMass-Lowell students coming for the bands and DJs. This is a big venue; there's two outdoor bars, a VIP lounge (call for reservations) and a great dance floor.

Food: The Blue Shamrock serves up traditional pub fare. Popular choices include the Steak Tips over Rice and Chicken Alfredo. Choose a lobster from the "You pick 'em, we steam 'em" lobster tank. There's always a few daily specials.

Entertainment: Live bands perform on Fridays. DJs entertain on Saturdays. There's plenty of TVs for sports fans; plus 2 pool tables, 4 dart boards and 2 Golden Tee Golf machines.

What's In A Name: The pub takes its name from its owners' nationalities: Greek and Irish.

The Claddagh

399 Canal Street, Lawrence
978.688.8337

open Mon - Thu 3:30pm 'til 1am, Fri noon 'til 2am,
Sat 2pm 'til 1am, Sun noon 'til 1am

The Claddagh has been a popular Merrimack Valley pub for almost 20 years. There's something here for all types of pub revelers. The bands that play here are quite good. They sponsor a yearly 5k road race and the Scully golf tournament which raises money for local charities. This is the area's top pool and dart pub. Very popular hang out for local softball teams.

Food: The Claddagh's menu is heavy on appetizers along with familiar pub choices like burgers and grilled dishes. The pizza here is great.

Entertainment: Wednesday is Open Mic Night. Bands entertain Thursdays, Fridays and Saturdays. There are TVs, including a 3 big screens for watching the games, 3 pool tables, 4 dart boards, a jukebox, Golden Tee Golf and other video games. Monday is Pool Night.

What's In A Name: Although now part of the city of Galway, Claddagh was once a fishing village located west of Galway city centre, just outside the old city walls where the Corrib River meets Galway Bay. Claddagh is famous for the Claddagh ring, whose design consists of two clasped hands holding a crowned heart, and symbolizes love, friendship and loyalty. The owner is from Sligo and he's as Irish as a man can be so he picked this lovely Irish symbol for his pub's name.

PubCorner.com

Connolly's

Logan Airport Hilton, East Boston
617.568.6700

open daily 11am 'til 12:30am

This "north of Boston" pub is actually located within the city of Boston; at Logan Airport. Connolly's is a large and handsome pub; the perfect escape for busy businessmen and women. An expert staff will relax you with friendly conversation and courteous service. All tastes are catered to with a large selection of beers, wines and cordials. You'll mingle with interesting travelers from around the world.

Food: Full lunch and dinner menu. An equally great spot for a quick snack or a full meal. Tasty appetizers, fresh salads, filling burgers and sandwiches plus much more.

Entertainment: Connolly's is a true conversation pub; it's a wonderful place for a good chat. They have 9 TVs and show all sporting events.

What's In A Name: The pub was named after Boston legend and sports hero James Brendan Connolly of South Boston; champion in the Triple Jump at the 1896 Olympics. A statue in Moakley Park depicts him at his competitive best.

The Dubliner

197 Market Street, Lowell
978.458.2120

open daily 11:30am 'til 2am

Opened over 35 years ago, The Dubliner is Lowell's oldest Irish pub. With its great food, entertainment and ambiance it has become a "meeting, dining and drinking tradition."

Food: The Dubliner serves up a wonderful mix of Irish and American favorites. The soups are homemade; and the pastas and seafood dishes are wonderful. Oh, and bring the kids; they have a terrific kids' menu as well.

Entertainment: Wednesday is Trivia Night. Bands entertain Thursday through Saturday. There are TVs for watching sporting events.

What's In A Name: Dubliner is great Irish name for a great Irish pub.

Harrington's

17 Water Street, Wakefield
781.245.1525

**Summer: Mon - Thu 4pm 'til 1am,
Fri - Sun 3pm 'til 1am
Winter: open daily 11:30am 'til 1am**

Harrington's is a cozy neighborhood pub, conveniently located in downtown Wakefield. An easy pit-stop for refueling after your walk around Lake Quannapowitt. They abhor grumpy people at Harrington's and promise to turn any frown upside-down with one of their their specialty cocktails (a superior pour at an agreeable price). Try the Nutty Irishman or the Chocolate Martini. A professional staff, a respected chef running the kitchen, a comfortable atmosphere, quality entertainment; Harrington's is fast becoming another Wakefield Landmark.

Food: Full menu; lunch and dinner. Dinner served from 4pm 'til 10pm with a light fare menu on Fri. and Sat. nights from 10pm 'til 11pm. Soups, salads, appetizers, burgers, sandwiches, sirloin tips, baked or broiled scrod, etc. Irish fare; Fish & Chips, Shepherd's Pie, Beef Stew, etc.

Entertainment: Every Wed. features traditional Irish Seisiun. Live music on Fri. and Sat. nights, the best local and international artists featuring traditional acoustic folk and classic rock.

What's In A Name: Harrington is the ancestral name of two sisters who are among the owners.

Honey Fitz

142 Pleasant Street, Malden
781.324.0111

**open Mon - Fri 11am 'til 2am,
Sun noon 'til Midnight**

Honey Fitz has been a Malden institution for over 20 years. They mostly cater to locals; but with the Malden Center Orange Line stop just a couple of hundred yards away it's an easy trip for visitors drawn by the great word of mouth this pub receives.

Food: Honey Fitz serves up a basic bar menu consisting of appetizers, sandwiches and burgers. Kitchen hours are 6pm 'til 10pm.

Entertainment: Trivia on Mondays. Wednesday is Karaoke night. Bar Pong on Thursdays. Live bands on Saturday. There's also a jukebox, video games and TVs for watching the games.

What's In A Name: John Francis "Honey Fitz" Fitzgerald was John F. Kennedy's maternal grandfather and also the Mayor of Boston from 1906-07 and again from 1910-14.

Hugh O'Neill's

45 Pleasant Street, Malden
781.338.9977

**open Mon - Wed 11am 'til 1am,
Thurs - Sat 11am 'til 2am,
Sun 10am 'til Midnight**

Hugh O'Neill's is a beautiful pub done out in mahogany and stained glass and features a working fireplace and plenty of nooks for private conversation. North Shore's largest vodka selection. Nice outdoor dining area.

Food: Hugh O'Neill's serves American cuisine along with some Irish favorites. The menu is leagues beyond pub grub. The Paninis and Pizzas are popular as are many dinner entrees such as Steak Tips, Fish & Chips and Grilled Salmon. Brunch and Irish Breakfast is served Saturday and Sunday 'til 4pm.

Entertainment: DJs entertain Thursday through Saturday and on holidays. Pub Quiz on Tuesday and Wednesday. Live bands are brought in on occasion. This is a great pub for watching sports on their big-screen and plasma TVs.

What's In A Name: The pub is named for Hugh O'Neill (1540 - 1616) who is best known for leading the resistance against England during the Nine Years War (1594 - 1603).

J.P. McBride's

27 Lafayette Square, Haverhill
978.469.8011

open daily 10:30am 'til 1am

J.P. McBride's is a handsome neighborhood pub that blends traditional design with modern practicality. Its designers utilized the calming effect of relaxed lighting and ample amounts of rich-dark wood to set the correct traditional ambience. A state of the art sound system, plasma TVs, Wi-Fi, and an advanced kitchen exceed all 21st century expectations. Combining the best of the old and the new is what inspired the pub's slogan, "A New Tradition." McBride's has an honest caring ownership, professional staff and fun loving regulars. They offer fantastic food, pour a gratifying pint and present some of the Merrimac Valley's best entertainment. With advanced reservations J.P. McBride's will host and cater functions and private parties.

Food: Classic American and traditional Irish cuisine; tasty appetizers, great salads, sandwiches, burgers and interesting entrees. Our favorites are the Fish & Chips and the Bangers & Mash. The perfectly prepared Reuben Sandwich is the house specialty.

Entertainment: Musicians performing a mix of styles or DJs entertain Thursday through Sunday. There are 4 plasma TVs for watching the games. Home of the J.P. McBride's Live Music Festival held each September. Free WiFi.

What's In A Name: In 1928 one of the pub owners' grandfather emigrated from Dingle to Boston and took a job in a blacksmith shop located in the Jamaica Plain (locally known as "JP") neighborhood of Boston on McBride Street. Eventually he took over the hammer and anvil and purchased the business. To be a blacksmith takes skill, dedication and lots of hard work. The same qualities are needed to run a great Irish Pub, hence the name J.P. McBride's.

PubCorner.com

Kelley's

75 South Main Street, Haverhill
978.374.0132

open Sun - Thu 11am 'til 1am,
Fri & Sat 11am 'til 2am

Kelley's is a cool little neighborhood watering hole that's in it's 7th decade of serving up good cheer to the people of Haverhill. They have a loyal clientele of good-spirited regulars.

Food: Kelley's serves lunch only. The menu is familiar pub grub. The burgers, hot dogs and steak tips are all very popular.

Entertainment: Live bands Fridays and Saturdays. 2 pool tables, a dart board, Golden Tee Golf, a great internet jukebox, and a TV at the bar.

What's In A Name: The pub was originally named "Kelly's" by it's owner, Kay Kelly. The pub has changed hands a few times. The second owner changed the name and the third owner wanted to go back to "Kelly's"....but Kay Kelly didn't want him to so he just added another "e."

Kilkenny Pub

660 Rogers Street, Lowell
978.441.9040

open Mon - Fri 11:30am 'til 2am,
Sat & Sun noon 'til 2am

A no stuffiness neighborhood pub, The Kilkenny is filled with local welcoming regulars. Proud of their personal service, the staff treats customers as part of the family. A laid back atmosphere and a gentle tab. An outdoor patio for warmer weather or if you care for a smoke. Pop into Kilkenny's; soothe your parched throat and escape the hustle and bustle of the daily grind.

Food: All the best pub fare. The tasty burgers are very popular. Great daily specials, baked haddock, steamers, etc. Always the freshest ingredients.

Entertainment: TVs including a big screen TV for the games, jukebox, darts. Golden Tee Golf, KENO.

What's In A Name: The owner's family is originally from the city of Kilkenny in southeast Ireland. Kilkenny is the Republic of Ireland's smallest city both in area and population and is Lowell's sister city.

Kitty O'Shea's

298 Cabot Street, Beverly
978.927.0300

open daily 11am 'til 1am

Kitty O'Shea's is a cozy little pub that attracts an interesting mix of characters: locals, college kids, teachers, etc. Authentic decor with a magnificent fireplace.

Food: Kitty O'Shea's serves an excellent selection of American and Irish fare. The menu includes Bangers & Mash, Guinness Beef Stew, Chicken Curry, homemade soups, salads, sandwiches and desserts. Traditional Irish Breakfast is served Saturday and Sunday.

Entertainment: Entertainment every night ranging from live bands to karaoke, traditional seisiún and pub quiz. Great place to catch the Premier League matches.

What's In A Name: Katherine Woods was born in 1846 in Bradwell, Essex, England, the daughter of an English chaplain. At the age of 22 she became the wife of Captain Willie O'Shea whom later became an Irish MP. In 1880 Kitty met Charles Stewart Parnell, an Irish nationalist who led the fight for Irish Home Rule in the 1880s. He is fondly remembered in Irish history as the "Uncrowned King of Ireland." In 1881 Kitty and Parnell began an affair that lasted 10 years and some argue that the affair prevented Irish Home Rule from being granted.

Major MagLeashe's

268 Washington Street, Salem
978.744.2328

open daily 11:30am 'til 1am

Major MagLeashe's is a popular Irish pub which attracts a wide cross section of North Shore residents and Salem tourists. Their burgers have been voted Salem's Best. The current owners, Paul Flaherty and Phil Shea hold the philosophy that a pub is a place where you don't have any problems, which is very evident here.

Food: The specialties at Major MagLeashe's are the burgers, BBQ Steak Tips, Pork and Chicken, Chowder and Chili. There are always daily specials.

Entertainment: There are 4 TVs, a jukebox, Golden Tee Golf and full service state lottery with KENO.

What's In A Name: The name MagLeashe was formed using the first three letters from each of the original three owners Irish names: Maguire, Leahey and Shea.

Molly Kay's

489 Middlesex Street, Lowell
978.441.1830

**open Mon - Fri 2pm 'til 2am,
Sat & Sun Noon 'til 2am**

If you're up for a dash of adventure this is the spot. Not another Irish pub cliché, Molly K's has more New York City attitude than Irish countryside appeal. Catering to a young (21 to 29) partying crowd, things get more wild as the night deepens. Superior cocktails served by pros without any moralizing. Molly K's keeps it interesting with great draft and drink specials. A more relaxed outdoor patio is available for quieter conversation. The late night stop for a hip, happening time.

Food: Molly's serves up a menu of tavern favorites. The burgers, steak tips and ribs are all very popular choices.

Entertainment: 2 pool tables, pool leagues. Darts. Live bands occasionally. 10 TVs for all the big games.

What's In A Name: The pub's two owners have nieces named Molly and Kay.

Molly's

173 Lewis Street, Lynn
781.593.6580

open daily 3pm 'til 2am

Molly's is a handsome pub in Lynn Center that's very popular with North Shore fun seekers.

Food: The menu at Molly's is familiar pub fare, with lots of sandwiches, burgers and grilled choices.

Entertainment: Live bands, DJ or Karaoke Thursday through Sunday. There are TVs to watch the games.

What's In A Name: Officially called Molly McMahon's; the owner named the pub after his granddaughter.

O'Hara's

1734 Lakeview Ave., Dracut
978.957.0271

open daily 11am 'til 2am

O'Hara's is an authentic Irish pub with a focus on sports. You'll party with a "wicked fun" staff that really loves this pub and truly cares for its customers. Regulars here become part of the O'Hara's Pub family. They even go on trips together. O'Hara's sponsors group outings to the Red Sox, deep-sea fishing, paintball, etc. You haven't lived until you've attended one of their theme nights: 70's parties, Mardi Gras, Hawaiian Luaus, etc. They also brag about having the cutest barmaids, especially the daytime staff - "these girls are hot." O'Hara's is a great time - guaranteed.

Food: Kitchen open Wednesday through Saturday serving up good quality pub grub. The Cajun Chicken Sandwich is great.

Entertainment: DJ on Saturdays. Plenty of TVs, including some big plasmas, for watching the games.

What's In A Name: They just picked a great Irish name for the bar.

The Old Court

29 Central Street, Lowell
978.452.0100

open Mon - Sat 'til 2am,
Sun 7pm 'til 2am

The Old Court is Lowell's premier Irish pub. Lots of artwork of Kanturk Castle adorn the walls. The entertainment at night takes place upstairs, at their Club Purgatory.

Food: The menu at The Old Court is Irish-American, leaning toward the Irish side of things. Some popular choices are the Shepherd's Pie and Fish & Chips. In fact, the Fish & Chips are known throughout the Merrimac Valley as being the best you'll find this side of Galway.

Entertainment: House Band on Thursdays. Occasional bands Friday and Saturday. There are TVs for watching the games; plus a dart board and MegaTouch video game.

What's In A Name: Kanturk Castle, an unfinished castle in County Cork, is also known as "The Old Court."

O'Neill's

120 Washington Street, Salem
978.740.8811

open Mon - Wed 11am 'til midnight,
Thu - Sun 11am 'til 1am

*Located in historic downtown Salem, O'Neill's
is a sharp looking pub that caters to all age
groups. They offer a relaxed atmosphere, great decor and the food is among the best on the North
Shore.*

Food: O'Neill's offers a wide ranging menu that includes traditional Irish dishes such as Shepherd's
Pie, Chicken Curry and Irish Stew along with popular cuisine including steaks and pastas.

Entertainment: Pub Trivia on Tuesday. Open Mic on Wednesday. DJ on Thursday. Traditional
Seusiun followed by a DJ on Friday. Live Irish Music Saturday and Sunday. There are plenty of TVs
for watching the games.

What's In A Name: The pub is named for Hugh O'Neill (1540 - 1616) who is best known for
leading the resistance against England during the Nine Years War (1594 - 1603).

The Peddler's Daughter

45 Wingate Street, Haverhill
978.372.9555

open daily 11am 'til 1am

*The Peddler's daughter is a lovely downstairs pub with
"country cottage" style - low ceilings and a cozy ambiance.
This is a pub to relax and spend some time in. Rated as
"Gourmet Greatness" by The Phantom Gourmet.*

Food: The Peddler's Daughter has an excellent menu chock full of hearty options. Some good picks
are the Peddler's Style Fish & Chips with homemade catsup, Guinness Beef Stew and Irish Style
Pork Bangers.

Entertainment: Pub Trivia on Tuesdays. Live music Thursday through Saturday plus some TVs
for the sports fans.

What's In A Name: Haverhill has had its share of successful business and professional people,
but it is doubtful that anyone was more widely known than Maggie Cline. Maggie was a vaudeville
star. Her father, Patrick, was a peddler.

The Pickled Onion

355 Rantoul Street, Beverly
978.232.3973

open daily 11am 'til 1am

The Pickled Onion, located in the heart of Beverly, is a busy bar, a quality restaurant, and a thriving nightspot. The pricing here will put a smile on your face, as will the caring staff.

Food: The Pickled Onion's food is considered traditional pub fare, consisting of half-pound Black Angus burgers, homemade soups, wraps, toasties, and pizzas. The Steaks Tips come highly recommended. Kids' menu available.

Entertainment: Trivia on Mondays. Open Mic on Tuesdays. Live music Wednesday through Saturday. Sunday is Guitar Hero Night. Big screen TV for the sports fans; plus a dart board.

What's In A Name: The name is kind of a play on words. A pickled onion, of course, is a food product; and "pickled" is slang for having had too much to drink.

Rosie O'Shea's

84 State Street, Newburyport
978.499.0606

open daily 11:30am 'til 1am

Boasting high quality food, reasonable prices, excellent service with a smile, and the best entertainment in the Merrimac Valley; Rosie O'Shea's is always a pleasurable experience.

Food: Casual dining, lunch and dinner. Interesting and tasty appetizers including Potato Pancakes and Fried Ravioli, fresh salads, soups including great Clam Chowder, sandwiches, burgers and fabulous entrees including Irish Whiskey Chicken and Herb Crusted Lamb Chops. There's always something new to try with unique daily specials at lunch and dinner. Irish Breakfast served 'til 2pm every Sunday.

Entertainment: DJs and bands Tuesday through Sunday. Irish Seisiun every Tuesday and Friday before the DJs take over.

What's In A Name: Rosie O'Shea was the long lost sister of the more famous Kitty O'Shea.

Stewart's

140 Jefferson Avenue, Everett
617.381.0563

open Mon - Sat noon 'til 1am,
Closed Sunday

Stewart's is settling in as one of the jewels of the north of Boston Irish pub scene. Occupying a building that's been a bar since 1919, they completely gutted the place and brought back that old time ambiance.

Food: Great pub menu with many homemade favorites like Shepherd's Pie, Beef Stew and Fish & Chips. Plus; burgers, sandwiches, seafood, steak tips and more.

Entertainment: Bands and DJs entertain on various nights. There are 3 TVs and 2 dart boards.

What's In A Name: The owner's last name is Stewart.

Sweeney's Retreat

18 Atlantic Avenue, Marblehead
781.631.6469

open Mon - Thurs 4pm 'til midnight,
Fri - Sat 11:30am 'til midnight,
Sun 9am 'til midnight

To most visitors from "back home" Sweeney's Retreat is reminiscent of a rural public house in Ireland. If you're tall watch your head on those 19th century beams.

Food: The menu at Sweeney's Retreat is Traditional American featuring a blend of appetizers, sandwiches and entrees. Sweeney's is best known for its fresh, native seafood dishes and aged choice sirloin beef. They also serve a great Traditional Irish Breakfast on Sunday.

Entertainment: There are TVs for watching sports. This pub is described as an "extreme talkfest." Occasional Karaoke and there's a Shuffleboard court.

What's In A Name: While in a Guinness induced trance the name Sweeney's Retreat was given to the pub's owner, Phil Sweeney, by a devil's angel. Phil is the former proprietor of Boston's famed Black Rose.

WEST OF BOSTON

Casey's Public House

81 Railroad Street, Holliston
508.429.4888

open Fri & Sat 11:30am 'til midnight,
Sun - Thu 11:30am 'til 11pm

Casey's is a fantastic little public house, a delightful spot to relax with friends and family. The historic Holliston Railway Depot has been renovated to house this pub. The depot was built in 1847 by Irish immigrant laborers for The Boston and Worcester Railway. Perfectly located near the town center, Casey's is easy to get to and there's lots of parking. The décor is a pleasant mix of Irish artifacts and sports memorabilia with large framed photos of Ted Williams and Babe Ruth overlooking all. The first floor is furnished with tall tables and chairs and features a long bar with plenty of seating. The second floor overlooks the bar area, and is more intimate with comfy leather couches, a few small tables and chairs and the pool table. Accessible ownership and a likable staff cater to the needs of easygoing patrons from the local area. Casey's is the quintessential neighborhood pub; so if you like pleasant people and a relaxed environment climb on board for a good time at Casey's Public House.

Food: Lunch and dinner bistro dining. Fresh salads, wings, pizza, a large variety of tasty burgers, chicken entrees, pasta dishes, fish and chips, etc.

Entertainment: A jukebox, pool table and large flat screen TVs covering all the sporting events.

What's In A Name: The pub is named after the Mighty Casey from the Ernest Thayer poem Casey At The Bat, first published on June 3, 1888. The town of Mudville described in the poem is actually a neighborhood in Holliston MA. This neighborhood is just feet from Casey's Public House. There you'll find a bronze statue of the "Mighty Casey."

Conley's

164 Belmont Street, Watertown
617.393.0237

open Mon - Sat 11:30am 'til 1am,
Sunday noon 'til Midnight

Conley's caters to a mix of really good folks from the surrounding Belmont / Watertown neighborhood. The pub will soon be expanding - more seating and more of the good times. The motto here is "Solid eats, decent times, cold brew...that's how we do."

Food: Conley's serves an excellent pub menu, which is quite extensive for a neighborhood bar. Pizzas are king at Conley's. Other selections include sandwiches, burgers, wraps, and grilled entrees. A new chef is expanding the menu. Daily specials offered.

Entertainment: Bands entertain once a week on either Thursday or Friday. There are TVs for sports fans and a good jukebox. The constant entertainment is the staff and patrons.

What's In A Name: The pub's owner is Stephen Conley.

Connery's Inn

102 Irving Street, Framingham
508.879.5981

open Mon-Sat 11am 'til 1am, Sun noon 'til 1am

Connery's has a relaxed atmosphere, with modest prices, and is filled with friendly people from the neighborhood. In business since 1911, the pub has been newly renovated, but hasn't lost its historic charm. New carpeting and comfy leather chairs have been added, the poolroom is now on the second floor, the patio has been refurnished and is a great place to chill during warm weather.

Food: Lunch and dinner, with a new expanded menu. Award-winning fare, known for their fabulous pizza! Cuisine made from scratch with the freshest and best ingredients. Great appetizers, salads, sandwiches, pasta dishes, burgers, and much more. You have to try their "Pubwich." They roll out pizza dough, fill it with hand-sliced ham, chicken, or hamburger, cover it with cheese, and add lettuce, tomato, and onion. Fold, slice and serve - ideal pub nourishment!

Entertainment: Live R&B bands on Thursday. Live Rock bands on Fridays. DJs on Saturday. Wednesday is charity Texas Hold 'Em poker night. Pool, plus 6 wide screen TVs covering all sporting events.

What's In A Name: The original owner was named Connery.

Donohue's

87 Bigelow Avenue, Watertown
617.924.4900

open Mon - Sat 8:30am 'til 1am,
Sun 9am 'til midnight

Donohue's brings you "Irish heritage with an American feel." Two large dining areas and a function room, the atmosphere encourages mingling. Named to Channel 4's "A List" as "Best Irish Pub In Boston" in 2006 and winner of a "Readers' Choice Award" as "Best Bar & Grill." Sponsor of the Donohue's Turkey Trot 5k road race, held every Thanksgiving to benefit the Watertown Boys & Girls Club.

Food: Donohue's menu is a mix of Irish and American pub fare with lots of good entree choices. The appetizers are said to be outstanding. One of the best Full Irish Breakfasts in the Boston area is offered on Weekends for only $10.

Entertainment: Trivia on Wednesday and Sunday. Live music Thursday through Sunday. This is a great venue for sports fans, with about a dozen big HD plasmas, a huge 100" HDTV, and many other TVs. Golden Tee Golf and WiFi internet access.

What's In A Name: The pub is named for its owner, John Donohue.

PubCorner.com

Dunn-Gaherin's

344 Elliot Street, Newton
617.527.6271

**open Mon - Sat 11am 'til midnight,
closed Sun**

Welcoming patrons for over 17 years, Dunn-Gaherin's is known as the most congenial location in Newton Upper Falls. This is a handsome and well designed establishment. There is a quaint bar area in front, and a warm, cozy dining room in the back. The decor features images of memorable local athletes and teams, most notably the sportsmen of Newton and Needham High Schools. There are over 30 beers available and also a great wine selection. Always-excellent service!

Food: The menu is quite extensive. Some favorites are the Handmade Brie Wontons appetizer, the Santa Fe Pasta and Tennessee Pork and the incredible Steak Tips served in a choice of sauces. Weekly specials are made from scratch and include Crab Cakes, Lasagna, Shepherd's Pie, and Beef Stew. There's a good selection of sandwiches and burgers and the homemade soups and chowders are outstanding. Curbside take-out is available. A late night menu is offered from 10: 30pm 'til 11:30pm.

Entertainment: Huge HD Flat-Screen TVs in the front bar for watching all the games. The staff is fun loving and known to entertain occasionally with a ditty or a joke. Live music during Saint Patrick's week.

What's In A Name: The pub is named for its proprietors, Robert Dunn and Seana Gaherin.

The Emerald Rose

785 Boston Road, Billerica
978.667.0500

open daily 11:30am 'til 1am

A handsome and impressive pub, The Emerald Rose is a fine place to meet friends for dinner and a pint, to entertain business clients, to host your lunch/dinner party or to just unwind after a trying day. The lively pub area is separate from the quieter, white tablecloth dining area. Outdoor dining is available on the patio in warmer weather.

Food: The Emerald Rose serves an American-Continental menu with many Irish dishes. Lunch is served 'til 4pm in the pub and the dining room. Dinner is served 'til 10pm. A late-night pub menu is served 'til midnight. Brunch is served Sundays 'til 2pm.

Entertainment: Tuesday is Trivia Night. There are numerous TVs carrying sporting events and live bands entertain occasionally.

What's In A Name: An allegorical name for Ireland, Emerald Rose is the english translation of Smaragraid Rós.

Fitzwilliam's Irish Pub

Burlington Marriott, One Mall Road, Burlington
781.229.6565

open Mon - Sat 11:30am 'til 1am,
Sun noon 'til 1am

Burlington's own Premier Irish Pub was built in Ireland, shipped to the states and reconstructed in the Marriott Hotel. It's a great re-creation; charming, cozy, and truly capturing the spirit of Ireland. Fitzwilliam's offers a great atmosphere, friendly service and a classic menu.

Food: Fitzwilliam's menu includes Irish favorites such as Shepherd's Pie, Lamb Stew, Potato & Bacon Soup, Fish & Chips, Pub Sandwiches and a great selection of Appetizers.

Entertainment: Karaoke on Wednesdays. TVs broadcast sporting events nightly. Monthly events include live bands.

What's In A Name: The pub is named after Fitzwilliam Square in Dublin, which is the last of Dublin's great Georgian squares, built between 1791 and 1825. Similar to Beacon Hill's Louisburg Square, Fitzwilliam Square is a prestigious residential address and the small park in its center is not open to the public, as it is the last remaining square where keys to the park gates are given only to residents.

J.J. McKay's

171 Commonwealth Rd., Wayland
508.651.3758

open Mon - Sat 8am 'til 11pm,
Sun 11am 'til 11pm

J.J. McKay's is a neighborhood pub with a casual atmosphere that's very popular with sports fans. There's a wonderful patio out back for lounging in spring or summer. Voted #1 in the Reader's Choice Awards for "Best Pub" and "Best Place For Lunch" and "Best Steak."

Food: The menu runs the gamut from steaks to seafood to Italian to regular pub grub; and they do it all well. There are specials every night including a few "neighborhood specials," where regular menu items are discounted. Sunday Brunch 'til 2pm. Catering and take-out available. For the full menu visit their website: www.JJMcKays.com

Entertainment: Live acoustic music on Saturdays. Great place for watching sports with 3 big screen and 5 regular TVs. They also have Golden Tee Golf and KENO.

What's In A Name: The owners are husband and wife John and Jean McKiernan. They're the two "J"s. "McKay" is a shortened version of McKiernan.

Kennedy's

247A Maple Street, Marlborough
508-485-5800

open Mon - Thu 11:30am 'til 10pm
Fri 11:30am 'til 10:30pm,
Sat noon 'til 10:30pm, Sun 1pm 'til 10pm

Kennedy's offers a warm, country-cozy ambiance. A cottage style decor makes you feel at home. The friendly atmosphere helps the conversation flow and reminds you that you're always among good friends here. Kennedy's Market, located in front of the pub, specializes fresh fish and meats and is committed to quality.

Food: Family dining. Comfortable home cookin' at very reasonable prices. Salads, great sandwiches, hearty burgers. Full course dinners with the best ingredients; fresh haddock, lobster, tender steaks, etc. Take-out and catering available.

Entertainment: The food is so fresh and delectable, the joy from your tastebuds will be entertainment enough.

What's In A Name: The owner's family name is Kennedy.

Mad Raven

841 Main Street, Waltham
781.894.8188

open Mon - Sat 11:30am 'til 1am,
Sun 11am 'til midnight

The Mad Raven combines a traditional cozy pub atmosphere with a modern style and top-notch cuisine. It offers a Boston-feel out on the Route 128 belt. The bartenders are terrific. Most have experience in Boston bars. The crowd is a mix of the people working on Bear Hill, techies, lawyers from the nearby courthouse and locals. Food, drink and good cheer...it's all here!

Food: The Mad Raven's selection of sandwiches, individual pizzas and entrees is great. The Steak Tips and the Maple Chicken Salad are both very popular choices.

Entertainment: Pub Quiz on Tuesday, Sports Quiz on Wednesday. Late night DJ on Thursday and Friday. The Mad Raven has a great sound system. They host the occasional Irish seisiún and you can catch all your favorite games on the big-screen TV.

What's In A Name: There's a raven in the family crest of one of the original owners.

Mickey Cassidy's

116 Main Street, Medway
508.533.1343

open Mon - Wed 4:30pm 'til midnight,
Thurs - Sat 11:30am 'til midnight,
Sunday Noon 'til midnight

Boasting some of the best craic in Metro West, Mickey Cassidy's features some of the best Irish music in the region. Open Mic night also reveals some surprising talents; and Mickey himself may treat you to a song or two.

Food: Mickey Cassidy's mixes a lot of Irish specialties in with its standard pub fare. Some good choices are the Sheehan's Swordfish, Mr. Murphy's Firehouse Chili and Waterford Chicken.

Entertainment: Live music Thursday through Saturday. Open Mic on Thursdays. TVs for watching the games.

What's In A Name: Mickey Cassidy is the pub's owner. Mickey says "Sláinte mhaith duit!" (Good health to you!).

Molly Malone's

1657 Worcester Road, Framingham
508.879.7200

open daily 11:30pm 'til 12:30am

Located in the Sheraton Hotel, Molly Malone's has a good reputation among pub afficionados in the Framingham area. The food is pretty good and the service is excellent. It's gets very lively whenever the Red Sox or Patriots are playing.

Food: Molly Malone's menu is a classic Irish-American mix of pub favorites. A great choice is the Skillet Seared Atlantic Salmon. There are always a few daily specials.

Entertainment: 7 TVs and a pool table (pool is free). They're likely to be adding live music on Fridays.

What's In A Name: Molly Malone was a famous personality who sold food, drink and good cheer in 19th century Dublin.

O'Hara's

1185 Walnut Street, Newton
617.965.6785

open Mon - Sat 11am 'til 11:30pm,
Closed Sun

O'Hara's is a classic neighborhood grille located in the heart of Newton Highlands. It offers a warm and welcoming atmosphere accented by dark wood, a sprawling horseshoe bar, and gracious paned windows that overlook Walnut Street. It was opened in 1985 and has built a loyal following of patrons who enjoy the food, spirits and company they always find at O'Hara's.

Food: O'Hara's offers good American and Italian cuisine at reasonable prices. The fare includes beef, seafood, chicken, pasta, pizzas and calzones. Try their famous Chicken Pot Pie served in a freshly baked loaf of bread.

Entertainment: Two TVs to watch all the games.

What's In A Name: O'Hara is the family name of the owners, John and Karl O'Hara.

Owen O'Leary's

319 Speen Street, Natick
508.650.1976

open Mon - Sat 11:30am 'til 12:30am,
Sunday 10am 'til 12:30am.

The third Owen O'Leary's, opened in 1996, serves not only the freshest food possible, but also the freshest beer. The restaurant / brewery serves its own handcrafted beers.

Food: Exceptional pub food is the standard fare at Owen O'Leary's with a robust selection of burgers, sandwiches, grilled entrees and pastas making up the menu. Brunch served on Sunday.

Entertainment: Plenty of TVs for sports fans, 2 pool tables, a dart board and about a half dozen video games.

What's In A Name: The owner's father's first name was Owen. His mother's maiden name was O'Leary.

Owen O'Leary's

50 Turnpike St. (Rt. 9 East), Southboro
508.481.1714

open daily 11:30am 'til 12:30am

This is the original Owen O'Leary's, which opened in 1989 in an area filled with chain restaurants. Owner Kevin Gill's mission was to provide the local people with a place where they could get a freshly prepared meal with a certain creativity and flair served in a cozy, comfortable pub atmosphere. Great rooftop patio.

Food: Exceptional pub food is the standard fare at Owen O'Leary's with a robust selection of burgers, sandwiches, grilled entrees and pastas making up the menu. Brunch served on Sunday.

Entertainment: Plenty of TVs for sports fans, 2 pool tables, and about a half dozen video games.

What's In A Name: The owner's father's first name was Owen. His mother's maiden name was O'Leary.

Paddy's

95 Elm Street, Newton
617.965.6444

open Mon - Sat 11:30am 'til Midnight,
Sunday Noon - 10pm

Paddy's has the look and feel of an old pub back in Ireland, with a custom-built mahogany bar, authentic irish furnishings, paned glass windows and an impressive decor. They cater mostly to their neighbors; and this is as much a restaurant as a bar, if not more.

Food: Paddy's has all the familiar lunch items like burgers, sandwiches, soups and salads. However, if you're hungry, their entrees are what you should try. The Beef Stew, Irish Country Side Shepherd's Pie and Baked Stuffed Haddock are outstanding.

Entertainment: TVs for watching the games. Celtic band occasionally on a Monday.

What's In A Name: The owners named their pub in honor of their father.

R.J. Crowley's

1391 Washington Street, Newton
617.527.5590

open Mon & Tue 4:30pm 'til 12:30am,
Wed - Fri 11:30pm 'til 12:30am,
Sat & Sun noon 'til 12:30am

RJ Crowley's is a great looking pub and restaurant with lovely pane glass windows and a dark mahogany decor. This place serves mostly local neighborhood types; but word is getting out about the good times and good food found here. New faces are constantly turning into regulars.

Food: RJ Crowley's serves a wonderful mix of pub classics and Irish specialties. The steak tips, turkey tips and seafood are all very popular. They also do an excellent Irish Mixed Grill and Shepherd's Pie. Daily specials.

Entertainment: Live music weekly and 5 TVs for the sports fans.

What's In A Name: The pub is named for its owner, Robert John Crowley.

The Skellig

240 Moody Street, Waltham
781.647.0679

**open Mon - Sat 11am 'til 1am,
Sun 11am 'til midnight**

*The Skellig is the creation of traditional
Irish musicians Tommy McCarthy and
Louise Costello. It serves fine food,
music and drink in a warm, friendly,
authentically Irish atmosphere.*

Food: The Skellig's menu includes sandwiches, burgers, Beef Stew, Fish & Chips and other pub favorites. The Bangers & Mash is said to be excellent here. Kids' menu available. Irish Breakfast and brunch served Saturday and Sunday 'til 3pm.

Entertainment: Pub Quiz on Monday. Live music, traditional Irish or cover bands, Tuesday through Sunday. TVs for watching the games.

What's In A Name: The Skellig Irish pub and restaurant is named after the Skellig Islands which lie in the Atlantic ocean 7 miles southwest of Valentia Island, County Kerry.

Stone's Public House

179 Main Street, Ashland   508.881.1778

**open Tue 11:30am 'til 12:30am,
Wed - Sat 11:30am 'til 1am,
Sun 10:30am 'til 1am, Closed Mon**

*Simply put; Stone's Public House is one of the
nicest establishments we visited during the
research for any of our books. Of more interest
is the "other thing" about Stone's; it's haunted.*
*Bizzare happenings have been documented over the years; lights and water taps turning themselves
on, doors that won't remain closed and "for no apparent reason" a handful of birdseed falling from
a hole in the ceiling.*

Food: One of the best menus in Metro West. Some good choices are the Seared Mustard Crusted Salmon and the Traditional Lamb Shepherd's Pie. For those of you looking for more standard pub fare, the toasted sandwiches are great. Brunch is served Sunday from 'til 2:30pm.

Entertainment: Irish seisiun every Tuesday and a regular blues jam on Sundays. Live bands on Fridays. Blue Grass is featured on the first and third Wednesday each month.

What's In A Name: The Stone family has a long history in the area, dating to 1635. John Stone opened the Railroad House, where Stone's Public House is located, in 1834.

Tommy Doyle's

349 Watertown Street, Newton
617.795.7201

open Mon - Wed 11:30am 'til midnight,
Thu & Fri 11:30am 'til 1am,
Sat 10:30am 'til 1am,
Sun 10:30am 'til midnight

The NewtonTommy Doyle's is a sharp looking intimate pub. It packs in the locals and is constantly building a wider clientele. They offer a good beer selection and the barstaff is among the best you'll find in the Boston area.

Food: The food at Tommy Doyle's is outstanding and covers a wide range from familiar pub grub to grilled entrees and seafood specialties. Want to stray a little from the norm at an Irish pub? Try their Fajitas and Enchilladas. You'll thank us. Brunch is offered on Saturday and Sunday.

Entertainment: Karaoke on Saturday. Live Blues on Sunday. There are TVs for watching the games and a great satellite music system.

What's In A Name: Tommy Doyle is a famous Kerry footballer who has earned seven All Ireland medals and captained the team in the 1986 final. A pub owner is a close friend of Tommy Doyle.

PubCorner.com

SOUTH OF BOSTON →

The Auld Sod

274 Washington St., Dedham
781.326.3957

open daily 11am 'til 1am

Opened in 1994 but completely renovated in 2005; The Auld Sod is a friendly and quite spacious neighborhood pub. There's a large, open area up front around the bar and a raised separate area in the back where the bands play.

Food: The Auld Sod's menu offers up quality American pub fare including burgers, sandwiches and grilled entrees. The Fish & Chips is excellent.

Entertainment: Karaoke, live bands and Pub Quiz on various nights. There are 6 TVs, 2 dart boards, plus Golden Tee Golf and video trivia.

What's In A Name: The Auld Sod refers to "the old country," and owner Hugh Varden gave his pub this name in honor of where he's from, County Clare.

The Banner

167 Union Street, Rockland
781.878.8717

open daily 11:00am 'til 1am

Located in Rockland center, The Banner is housed in a 120 year old building rich in local history. As they say, "Come savor the history of Rockland and the Irish." They have a nice private function room called McGuire's Snug.

Food: The Banner's menu includes a good mix of Irish, Italian and seafood favorites. The BBQ and fresh Lobsters are great. They do a wonderful Irish Breakfast. The kitchen is open 'til 10pm.

Entertainment: Live Irish and varied entertainment every night. Blues Jam on the last Saturday of each month.

What's In A Name: The Banner is a nickname for County Clare in Ireland.

Beckett's

1065 Main Street, Walpole
508.668.1191

open daily noon 'til 1am

Formerly The Kylemore, this pub was recently taken over by the experienced hand of John Jacob (Napper Tandy's in Norwood) and what a wonderful re-birth this spot has undergone with Beckett's. It's an ample sized pub, but not at the expense of intimacy; it's decor touches upon elegance while maintaining a casual vibe. Although in its early days, Beckett's has already established itself as one of the pub jewels in Greater Boston.

Food: Beckett's menu consists of hearty pub fare including Irish favorites along with seafood, stir fry, fajitas and pizza. Some great choices are the Irish Peppered Steak and the Country Fried Chicken. Full menu served 'til 10pm, then you can get appetizers 'til 11pm and pizzas 'til midnight. How about a late-night Beckett's Big Five Pizza? Now that'll fill you up before bed.

Entertainment: Tuesday is Dart Night. Trivia on Wednesday. Karaoke on Thursday. TVs for watching all your favorite sporting matches.

What's In A Name: The pub is named for Irish playwright, novelist and poet Samuel Beckett, winner of the 1969 Nobel Prize for literature.

Brennan's

402 Turnpike Street, South Easton
508.238.3773

open Mon - Fri 4pm 'til Midnight,
Sat & Sun 11:30am 'til 1am

Brennan's Grille & Irish Tavern is a spacious pub with a cozy feel. They offer great food, a vast beer selection, full bar with great martini and wine lists, and one of the best single-malt scotch selections you'll find.

Food: Brennan's has a terrific menu with a wide selection of fresh seafood, hand-cut steaks, pastas, chicken and traditional Irish dishes such as Irish Chicken Pie, Dublin Sandwich, Irish Wedges and Corned Beef & Cabbage.

Entertainment: Live bands entertain Thursday through Sunday; with Sunday set aside for traditional seisiun. 3 plasma TVs for watching the games plus KENO.

What's In A Name: The pub is named after its owner, Steve Brennan.

C.B. O'Hanley's

275 North Main Street, West Bridgewater
508.436.7860

open daily 11am 'til 1am

C.B. O'Hanley's is a beautiful pub; newly opened and totally renovated. Well designed with lots of comfortable seating. Totally unblemished, this is one of the most pristine pubs we've been to. A great atmosphere for groups of all ages; an affable staff caters to your every need and you'll mingle easily with good-natured patrons.

Food: Lunch and Dinner (same menu). Delicious pub menu featuring fresh salads, delicious sandwiches, juicy steaks and fantastic pizza.

Entertainment: Live entertainment every night of the week. Texas Hold 'Em Poker (just for fun) every Sunday at 3:30pm. Stand-up comedy on Tuesday. Wednesday is Open-Mic night with great amateur performers. Friday and Saturday the most talented bands play live, original music and classic rock.

What's In A Name: This pub is named in honor of the owner's son.

Chieftain

23 Washington Street, Plainville
508.643.9031

open daily 11am 'til 12:30am

Established by Tom and Mary Cahill in 1995, The Chieftain is the only authentic Irish pub in the immediate area and a cornerstone of the local Irish community.

Food: The Chieftain offers a wide menu of traditional Irish and classic American fare specializing in seafood. Try the Lismore Shepherd's Pie or the Baked Stuffed Haddock. Mary's Brown Bread is baked fresh each day and served with every meal.

Entertainment: Live bands, mostly Irish, entertain on Friday and Saturday nights. They host a Pub Quiz. There's Golden Tee Golf, a jukebox and 3 TVs plus a big screen.

What's In A Name: The pub is named in honor of the Irish musical group The Chieftains.

Concannon's Village

60 Lenox Street, Norwood
781.762.2232

open daily 11am 'til 12:30am

Concannon's is a great pub to meet friends for conversation or to watch the game. Extremely inexpensive, Concannon's is happy to be known as the most pocket-friendly pub in the area. They attract patrons of all ages. The crowds are easygoing, fun and very well behaved. The Concannon's Village Hall holds over 300 people comfortably and is available for functions and special events.

Food: Lunch and Dinner. A hearty pub menu featuring tasty sandwiches, salads, burgers, pork-chops, steak-tips, served with a generous amount of fries or onion-rings.

Entertainment: A fantastic pub for watching a sporting event. Flat screen TVs and 4 big screens assure a clear view of the game. They also have a jukebox with all your old rock favorites.

What's In A Name: Concannon is the owner's family name.

Doyle's

956 Washington St., South Easton
508.238.9061

open Mon-Wed 11am 'til 11pm,
Thu-Sat 11am 'til 1am,
Sun Noon 'til 11pm

Doyle's is a very friendly pub and restaurant that serves up some of the best food and cheer south of the city. They boast one of the finest waitstaffs in the area.

Food: Doyle's Bar & Grill offers a wide selection for hungry diners; including seafood, grilled entrees, stir fry, pizzas, deli sandwiches and fajitas. The highlight here, in our opinion, is the seafood. Always fresh and expertly prepared; and the raw bar is magnificent. Children's menu available.

Entertainment: A whole bunch of TVs facing every which way so you can follow the game from wherever you're sitting.

What's In A Name: The pub is named for it's owners, Kenny and Tom Doyle.

Finnegan's Wake

7 Glenwood Avenue, Walpole
508.668.1189

open daily 11:30am 'til 12:30am

Earthy tones, easy lighting, a cozy atmosphere and friendly people; Finnegan's Wake fits the definition of a great Irish pub. Situated about a half-hour south of Boston; this pub makes for a nice stop on your way to or from Gillette Stadium or the Wrentham Village Outlets. Nice function room for up to 120 people.

Food: Traditional favorites include Shepherd's Pie, Bangers & Mash, Guinness Pie and Mixed Grill. The 'special board' includes items such as Prime Rib, Filet Mignon, Grilled Pork Chops, Stuffed Haddock and Chicken Marsalla. Unique specials are offered for both lunch and dinner.

Entertainment: Live bands perform in the bar and function room on weekends. Finnegan's Wake occasionally does a Comedy Dinner show. Darts available.

What's In A Name: Finnegan's Wake is a play by famed Irish writer James Joyce. It is also the favorite song of the pub's owner.

Galway Pub

58 Court Street, Plymouth
508.746.6452

open daily 10:00am 'til 1am

Holders of the oldest liquor license in town; The Galway is a clean and comfortable little pub located in historic Plymouth center; not far from Plymouth rock.

Food: No kitchen but bar snacks are available.

Entertainment: 2 TVs, a jukebox, Golden Tee Golf and other video games.

What's In A Name: The mother of pub owner Gerald Rooney was from Galway, on Ireland's west coast. Galway is Ireland's 3rd largest, and fastest growing, city.

Hillside Pub

2 Royal Avenue, Canton
781.828.7778

open Mon - Sat 8:30am 'til 1am,
Sun noon 'til 1am

The Hillside Pub is an honest little public house with an attentive staff and altruistic ownership. They keep their flock happy by offering an impressive pour at a reasonable price. Both Dunkin Donuts and Reebok headquarters are located just up the road making The Hillside a great after work gathering spot. Who knew donuts and athletic wear would mingle so well?

Food: Full pub menu featuring burgers, sandwiches, Steak Tips, Shepherd's Pie, Irish Stew, roast turkey dinners, daily specials and much more. The soups are homemade and The Hillside serves some of the best burgers South of Boston.

Entertainment: Trivia on Mondays. Live music most Saturdays (call for schedule). Plasma TVs, Darts, jukebox, Golden Tee Golf.

What's In A Name: The pub is located at the foot of the beautiful Blue Hills.

Kelly's Landing

159 Bridge Street, Weymouth
781.335.9899

open daily 11:30 'til 1am

Kelly's is an unpretentious spot that's a haven for local seafood lovers. Most of the space here is dedicated to the restaurant side of things, with an open kitchen in the back. The pub area is a smaller side room where neighborhood types gather daily to exchange banter and cheer on their favorite teams.

Food: Kelly's is best known for its seafood. Everything is fresh and expertly prepared. If you're in the mood for some beef we recommend the Steak Mafia; it's truly out of this world.

Entertainment: Karaoke on Saturday nights. There are TVs for the sports fans, plus a great jukebox and KENO.

What's In A Name: The original Kelly's Landing was opened by Larry and Ma Kelley in 1927 on South Boston's City Point shoreline. A mention of the original Kelly's to Southie old-timers will evoke a flow of old memories of walking the South Boston Strandway on a date with a "French Fry" and topping off the evening with an ice cream cone. The original location is etched in history and memorialized by the continued Kelly's tradition. The name is also landmarked on Coast Guard maps as an official site.

Maguire's

503 Foundry St., South Easton
508.230.8888

open Mon - Sat 11am 'til 1am,
Sun Noon 'til 1am

Maguire's is Easton's oldest independently owned and operated restaurant and bar. They offer reasonable prices and a comfortable atmosphere.

Food: Maguire's is known for its quality food. The menu includes a wide selection of starters, salads and sandwiches; about a dozen main courses including beef, pork, chicken and seafood entrees (the Roast Turkey Dinner is great!) and even a few pizza choices. There are lunch and dinner specials each day.

Entertainment: Several TVs for watching the games and a good cable radio system.

What's In A Name: Jack Maguire is the godson of one of the pub's owners.

McGreal's

690 Main Street, Norwell
781.659.9303

open daily 11:30am 'til midnight

At the address previously occupied by The Captain's Quarters, McGreal's is a comfortable and casual South Shore tavern that's been building up a good reputation for itself. During the winter you can stomp the snow off your shoes on the porch and settle in by the fireplace to relax.

Food: McGreal's offers a pub-style selection of appetizers, sandwiches and pizzas. The Specialty Pizzas are quite good; particularly the Tavern Special, for meat lovers. The kitchen is closed on Mondays.

Entertainment: Open Mic Wednesday and Saturday nights. They have 5 TVs for watching your favorite sports, 2 dart boards, a pool table, Golden Tee Golf and a jukebox. Meat Raffle on Sundays.

What's In A Name: The pub is named after the owner's daughter, Maryann McGreal.

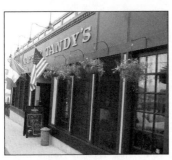

Napper Tandy's

46 Day Street, Norwood
781.762.0032

open Mon - Sat 11am 'til 1am,
Sun noon 'til 1am

Natural, neat and homey, this pub could be found in any Irish village. A large bar area for craic, a quieter area for dining, and a lovely outdoor patio filled with flowers for the warmer months. An affectionate waitstaff and professional pintsmiths care for your needs. With great food, a neighborly atmosphere and a banner staff Napper Tandy's has decoded the secret behind a true Irish Pub.

Food: A full lunch and dinner menu. Salads, sandwiches, burgers, chicken and steak entrees. Pleasing and flavorful - plentiful plates at puny prices.

Entertainment: Challenge yourself and your mates on Wednesday with Napper Tandy's Pub Quiz. Enjoyable live music Thursday and Sunday.

What's In A Name: James "Napper" Tandy was a famous late 18th century Irish patriot. He attacked municipal corruption, proposed to boycott English goods because of restrictions they placed on Irish commerce and aided in the founding of the United Irish Society. His story lives on in the Irish ballad "The Wearing of the Green."

Nutty Irishman

579 West Street, Bridgewater
508.378.7626

open Sun - Thu 11am 'til midnight,
Fri & Sat 11am 'til 1am

The Nutty Irishman is a large pub with a comfortable and relaxed attitude. This is a favored haunt for local merrymakers in the Bridgewater area. They also draw loyal pubbers from nearby Bridgewater State College. Mostly a sports pub, but they offer a nod to the Irish with some "green" decor and traditional menu items.

Food: The Nutty Irishman serves up a wide ranging menu of familiar pub favorites along with Irish classics. Most popular are the burgers and pizzas. They also boast of serving some of the best Clam Chowder south of Boston.

Entertainment: More than enough TVs to satisfy the most zealous sports fan. There are 3 pool tables, darts, a jukebox and KENO.

What's In A Name: The owner's wanted a fun, wacky name for their pub and this is what they came up with. It's not so nutty; a Nutty Irishman is actually a drink made with Kalhua, Bailey's and coffee with whipped cream.

O'Donnell's

1048 North Main Street, Randolph
781.963.9812

open Sun noon 'til 1am, Mon 11am 'til 1am,
Thu - Fri 10am 'til 1am, Sat 11am 'til 1am

O'Donnell's is a fun roadside tavern that offers good, generous meals with a smile. A popular stop for Randolph locals for lunch and dinner and merrymakers into the evening. They brag of serving the "coldest beer in town." Caring, hands-on management by the O'Donnell family ensures a good time.

Food: O'Donnell's offers up hearty and filling American tavern fare. They're known for their great Steak Tips. There's a good selection of appetizers and they make a really nice barroom-style pizza.

Entertainment: Plasma TVs, jukebox, Golden Tee, video bowling and KENO.

What's In A Name: This pub is named for the family which owns and operates it.

Olde Irish Alehouse

2 Bridge Street, Dedham
781.329.6034

open Mon - Thu 4pm 'til 1am,
Fri 3pm 'til 1am, Sat & Sun noon 'til 1am

A Dedham institution situated on the Charles River, The Olde Irish Alehouse offers water-view dining in an intimate, warm setting. There's a big, elegant function room (Waterford Place) available for private parties.

Food: The menu consists of American and Irish favorites along with traditional pub grub. Some good choices are the Alehouse Steak, Irish Farmhouse Chicken Pie and Baked Scrod. Daily specials are offered.

Entertainment: Trivia on Tuesdays. Karaoke Wednesday and Sunday. Live bands Thursday through Saturday. There are numerous TVs for catching your favorite sporting events.

What's In A Name: The pub has the ambiance of an old, traditional Irish alehouse.

Owen O'Leary's

1280 Belmont Street, Brockton
508.584.2221

open Mon - Sat 11:30am 'til 1am,
Sunday 10am 'til 1am.

The second Owen O'Leary's, opened in 1992, is the perfect combination of atmosphere and size. It's large enough to accommodate most functions and events while still preserving that pub feel.

Food: Exceptional pub food is the standard fare at Owen O'Leary's with a robust selection of burgers, sandwiches, grilled entrees and pastas making up the menu. Brunch served on Sunday.

Entertainment: Plenty of TVs for sports fans, 2 pool tables, a dart board and about a half dozen video games.

What's In A Name: The owner's father's first name was Owen. His mother's maiden name was O'Leary.

The Paddock

998 East Main Street, Walpole
508.668.2774

Open Mon - Sat 11:30am 'til 1am,
Sun noon 'til 12:30am

The Paddock is a "Cheers-like" pub to neighbors and folks from the surrounding towns. They offer great food and drink, terrific live music, and fun times. Three females manage this place and the customers really dig that.

Food: The Paddock offers a full lunch and dinner menu of pub favorites, Irish fare and delicious entrees.

Entertainment: Live entertainment Thursday through Saturday. Dart league on Tuesday nights. There are 8 TVs for watching the games with a free buffet during Patriots' halftime. Nice computer jukebox and KENO.

What's In A Name: A paddock is where the horses are housed at a race track. The owners picked this name for good luck.

Red Rose Café

800 East Broad Street, Weymouth
781.337.3322

Open daily 10am 'til 1am

Weymouth's Red Rose Café is a lovely little neighborhood pub, cozy and quaint. They boast a terrific staff and friendly patrons. The food servings are large, the pour is generous, and the prices are most agreeable... You'll be at home in the Red Rose Café.

Food: The Red Rose serves lunch and dinner daily. Great pub grub, steaks, burgers, sandwiches etc. They also have wonderful nightly specials featuring fresh fish dinners, home style roast turkey, sirloin tips, etc.

Entertainment: Occasionally DJs and live bands perform. They have a dartboard and all the games on TV.

What's In A Name: The pub was named for the song "The Red Rose Café" by popular Irish group The Fureys. The song is about a wonderful pub near Amsterdam and as its closing line says: "...So pull up a chair and forget about life; it's a good thing to do now and then. And if you like it here I have an idea; tomorrow let's all meet again."

Shamrock Pub

175 Railroad Avenue, Norwood
781.762.9717

open Mon - Sat 10am 'til 1am, Sun Noon 'til 1am

A true neighborhood pub; at The Shamrock you'll convene with the area's most colorful personalities. Extremely inexpensive, good-mood prices, it's almost a pleasure paying for a pint. The Guinness has been flowing here for a long time; three generations of the same family have held master over the tap. The building is over a hundred years old and holds onto every bit of its character; you can sense the good times it has absorbed over the years. As Shamrock pub legend has it; one pint enjoyed here leads to a year's good luck. Many of the Shamrock's patrons have enough "luck" for several lifetimes.

Food: The Shamrock is a popular lunch spot with tasty pub fare. Customers rave about the burgers.

Entertainment: Pool, big screen TV for the games. Live bands play and seisiun occasionally.

What's In A Name: The family's grandmother named the pub in honor of her Irish heritage.

The Snug

114 North Street, Hingham
781.749.9774

open daily 6am 'til Midnight

The Snug's motto is "Home Of The Perfect Pint" but to us it may as well be "Home Of The Perfect Pub." State of the art European draft system assures a great pour every time. This is quickly becoming a favorite haunt for many South Shore Irishmen.

Food: The Snug's menu is typical American pub fare with familiar Irish favorites. The Shepherd's Pie, Fish & Chips and homemade soups are excellent. Much of their menu is homemade. Breakfast, including Traditional Irish Breakfast, is served every day.

Entertainment: Seisiun on Mondays. Live musicians Wednesday through Saturday playing folk, blues, rockabilly and acoustic. Some of the best known Irish musicians make a stop at The Snug when visiting Boston.

What's In A Name: A snug is an intimate, enclosed booth at a pub; a friendly nook to which someone might retreat or retire for seclusion and comfort...or to snuggle with their honey.

Squire's

1202 Washington Street, Hanover
781.826.3360

open Mon - Sat 11am 'til 1am,
Sun noon 'til 1am

Somewhat off the beaten path, Squire's is an oasis that caters to all types; from construction workers to white collar professionals to retirees. It always seems to be bustling here; a beehive of activity and cheer. Often the road less traveled is well worth the trip. In this case that road is Route 53 in Hanover.

Food: Squire's offers up terrific pub fare. The burgers are among the best in the Boston area. Good selection of steaks and grilled options. They serve a pretty good pizza pie at Squire's too.

Entertainment: 6 TVs, darts, jukebox, video bowling. Live music on Saint Patrick's Day.

What's In A Name: In feudal times a squire was a man-at-arms in the service of a knight, often as his apprentice. In later years, the term's meaning reversed and the knight was in the service of the squire. That's all pretty interesting, but it's got nothing to do with the pub's name. The owner's last name is Squire.

PubCorner.com

CAPE COD & THE ISLANDS

Bobby Byrne's

345 Rt. 28 (489 Bearses Way), Hyannis
508.775.1425

open daily 11am 'til 1am

The authentic neighborhood pubs and saloons of New York City were the inspiration behind the Bobby Byrne's pubs. Bobby Byrne created his pubs as a poet constructs a poem; each with its own plot and theme; it's own structure, style, rhythm and rhyme. A Bobby Byrne's pub offers an unpretentious social environment, natural, relaxed and fun. At this pub you'll mingle with a variety of patrons. They say their pub is like Noah's Ark, with every type of person in the society represented. The hands-on management and exceptional staff generate the perfect pub atmosphere. We were told Bobby Byrne's pubs are proper pubs, fitting the classic sense of the word public, a place with universal appeal, a microcosm of the society. After visiting Bobby Byrnes Pubs we realized they have developed pub utopia.

Food: Eclectic American fare with an emphasis on fresh local seafood. Appetizers like the Sesame Encrusted Ahi Tuna, coated with black and white sesame seeds, pan-seared rare and served chilled on a bed of mandarin coleslaw with ginger soy sauce and wasabi. Original salads such as the Shenanigan: Grilled garlic shrimp & marinated steak tips with a mixed green salad, Swiss cheese & croutons. For a delicious entree try the Seafood Sauté: Mussels, sea scallops & shrimp sautéed with diced fresh tomatoes in a garlic & wine lemon butter sauce, served over fettuccini.

Entertainment: Satellite broadcasts of all national and international sporting matches.

What's In A Name: The pub is named for its founder Bobby Byrne. A "people-pub" expert, Mr. Byrne tended bar in New York City and Los Angeles for 25 years before coming to Cape Cod and opening his first pub in Mashpee in July of 1973. The full story is available online at www.bobbybyrnes.com.

Bobby Byrne's

Routes 28 & 151, Mashpee
508.477.0600

open daily 11am 'til 1am

The authentic neighborhood pubs and saloons of New York City were the inspiration behind the Bobby Byrne's pubs. A Bobby Byrne's pub offers an unpretentious social environment, natural relaxed and fun. At this pub you'll mingle with a variety of patrons. The hands-on management and exceptional staff generate the perfect pub atmosphere. After visiting Bobby Byrnes Pubs we realized they have developed pub utopia.

Food: Eclectic American fare with an emphasis on fresh local seafood. Appetizers like the Sesame Encrusted Ahi Tuna. Original salads such as the Shenanigan: Grilled garlic shrimp & marinated steak tips with a mixed green salad, Swiss cheese & croutons. For a delicious entree try the Seafood Sauté: Mussels, sea scallops & shrimp sautéed with diced fresh tomatoes in a garlic & wine lemon butter sauce, served over fettuccini.

Entertainment: Satellite broadcasts of all national and international sporting matches.

What's In A Name: The pub is named for its founder Bobby Byrne. A "people-pub" expert, Mr. Byrne tended bar in New York City and Los Angeles for 25 years before coming to Cape Cod and opening his first pub in Mashpee in July of 1973. The full story is available online at www.bobbybyrnes.com.

Bobby Byrne's

Route 6A & Tupper Road, Sandwich
508.888.6088

open daily 11am 'til 1am

Bobby Byrne created his pubs as a poet constructs a poem; each with its own plot and theme; it's own structure, style, rhythm and rhyme. A Bobby Byrne's pub offers an unpretentious social environment, natural, relaxed and fun. They say their pub is like Noah's Ark, with every type of person in the society represented. The hands-on management and exceptional staff generate the perfect pub atmosphere. We were told Bobby Byrne's pubs are proper pubs, fitting the classic sense of the word public, a place with universal appeal, a microcosm of the society.

Food: Eclectic American fare with an emphasis on fresh local seafood. Appetizers like the Sesame Encrusted Ahi Tuna. Original salads such as the Shenanigan. For a delicious entree try the Seafood Sauté.

Entertainment: Satellite broadcasts of all national and international sporting matches.

What's In A Name: The pub is named for its founder Bobby Byrne. A "people-pub" expert, Mr. Byrne tended bar in New York City and Los Angeles for 25 years before coming to Cape Cod and opening his first pub in Mashpee in July of 1973. The full story is available online at www.bobbybyrnes.com

Cape Cod Claddagh

77-79 West Main St., West Harwich
508.430.2440

Open each day Noon 'til 1am

The Copper Top Tavern is the pub of the Cape Cod Claddagh Inn; which is a Victorian Inn reminiscent of a small Irish manor house. The pub is a delightfully cozy and intimate; authentic in every detail.

Food: Full menu including all your pub favorites with a few specials offered each day.

Entertainment: Irish music occurs spontaneously at The Claddagh. Bring your own instrument or use one from the pub's walls. Live music daily including Cape Cod's oldest Traditional Seisiún on Saturdays.

What's In A Name: Although now part of the city of Galway, Claddagh was once a fishing village located west of Galway city centre, just outside the old city walls where the Corrib River meets Galway Bay. Claddagh is famous for the Claddagh ring, whose design consists of two clasped hands holding a crowned heart, and symbolizes love, friendship and loyalty.

Cape Cod Irish Village

512 Main St., West Yarmouth
508.771.0100

open daily noon 'til 1am

Established in 1976, the "Village" offers comfortable guest rooms, a restaurant and Irish Pub. Whatever you're looking for - nearby beaches, boating, golf or just great Irish charm; the "Village" delivers.

Food: Breakfast 'til 11am. Dinner 5pm 'til 8:30pm. Soups, Salads, Sandwiches, Wonderful fresh seafood (broiled, baked, or fried). Delectable steaks and chops. A splendid "Blas Na h Eireann" (taste of Ireland) selection with all the best Irish Dishes.

Entertainment: Absolutely the best in Traditional Irish Music, almost every night of the entire year in season. Music starts at 8:30 pm every night. In the off-season live music is offered on weekends.

What's In A Name: True Irish village hospitality on beautiful Cape Cod.

Cape Cod's Irish Pub

126 Main St., West Harwich
508.432.8808

Summer Hours: Tue - Sun 8pm 'til 1am, Closed Mon

A pub for the masses, colorful pubbers of all ages and nationalities let their guard down and create a festive environment. The polls are in... 95% of the guests of The Cape Cod Irish Pub have a fantastic experience....the other 5% have a super-fantastic experience.

Food: No kitchen.

Entertainment: A pool table and darts are available, but patrons gather here for top-notch live entertainment 6 nights a week. Karaoke Tuesday and Sunday (an exhibition of amusement). Wednesday features gratifying Irish tunes. Thursday is a mix of Irish and rock hits. Friday delivers stellar acts performing popular covers. Saturday is Irish sing-a-long night, a monumentally social experience.

What's In A Name: It's on Cape Cod and it's an Irish pub... duhhh!

Doyle's

1329 Route 28, South Yarmouth
508.760.1000

open daily 11:30am 'til 1am

Doyle's is more of a dining establishment than drinking location, known for great food and great people. Country cottage comfortable with separate dinning and bar areas. Their outdoor patio is heated and open year-round. A relaxed atmosphere, huge portions, wallet friendly pricing and a respectable pour is why Doyle's is one of the Mid-Cape's most popular public houses.

Food: Homemade dishes created using the finest and freshest ingredients. Salads, soups and chowders, sandwiches, burgers, popular steak and seafood dishes. Always family friendly, early bird specials, take-out available. A favored lunch location.

Entertainment: The good company of a caring staff and their friendly customers.

What's In A Name: A great Irish name; the pub's always been called Doyle's, it's the family name.

Kitty Murtagh's

4 West Creek Road, Nantucket
508.325.0781

open daily 11:30am 'til 1am

Kitty Murtagh's is a social hub for the Island of Nantucket. It oozes pub authenticity. The decor is a fun collection of Irish antiques and knicknacks which underscore the light, casual atmosphere that Kitty's fosters. Generosity abounds here; from the portions of their hearty fare to the welcoming spirit right down to your pint of Guinness; because that "pint" will be properly poured and served in a 20oz. glass.

Food: Kitchen open 'til 9:30pm. The menu includes filling pub favorites and traditional Irish dishes. The Kitty's Triple Tenderloin is something special. The seafood is the freshest you'll find and there are seafood specials nightly.

Entertainment: Traditional Irish musicians, local bands and DJs entertain on weekends. There are 2 pool tables, dart boards, and plenty of TVs for sports fans.

What's In A Name: The pub is named after owner John Keane's grandmother.

Liam Maguire's

273 Main St., Falmouth
508.548.0285

open Mon - Sat 11:30am 'til 1am,
Sun Noon 'til 1am

The perfect Irish pub found in an ideal setting: beautiful Falmouth on historic Cape Cod. Soak up the sun then soak up true Irish atmosphere. You will easily mingle with joyful people of all ages. Rich with craic, the best entertainment, fantastic food and service to match. We have a monumental crush on Liam Maguire's.

Food: The menu offers all the traditional Irish classics and a wide range of international dishes. Fantastic selection of fresh seafood dishes. Some great choices are the Sesame Swordfish Steak and the Irish Whiskey Steak Tips.

Entertainment: Internationally famous bands play Irish and American folk seven nights a week. 10 screens deliver all the sports action to the fans.

What's In A Name: The pub is owned by Liam and Deborah Maguire. Liam, raised in Castle Derg, County Tyrone, has traveled Europe, Canada, and the United Sates as a professional entertainer for over thirty years.

Molly's

585 Main Street, West Yarmouth
508.778.1927

open daily 7:30am 'til 1am

A lovely restaurant and a handsome bar. The pub is separated from the dining room; this creates a good atmosphere for both dining and socializing. A good crowd of all ages mingles easily. Leave your anxieties at home; enjoy fantastic food and a wonderful pub at Molly's.

Food: Breakfast, Lunch and Dinner. Great Chowder, salads, soups, sandwiches, steaks, seafood. Irish dishes, American specialties, Italian favorites, and a bit of everything to please all tastes. Winner of the 2005 Cape Cod Chowder Competition.

Entertainment: Live music Friday and Saturday nights. 3 pool tables, darts, jukebox, Golden Tee Golf, all the games on TV plus the GA Games.

What's In A Name: The pub's name is short for Molly Malone from the old Irish tune, but no need for last names here...everyone is on a first name basis.

O'Shea's Olde Inne

348 Main Street, West Dennis
508.398.8887

open Sun - Thu 4:30pm 'til midnight,
Fri & Sat 4:30pm 'til 1am

O'Shea's is perhaps the lovliest pub in our book and a "must visit" for pub lovers of all stripes. Whether your passion is food, music, or the craic that flows expertly from both the tap and the bartender; O'Shea's will impress. Located in the home built by Captain Coleman Studley in 1850, it's said that the ghost of the captain haunts the pub. We certainly can't blame him for staying.

Food: O'Shea's menu is loaded with fresh seafood options. You'll find some of the best seafood on The Cape here. The Baked Sea Scallop Casserole is fantastic. There are also traditional choices such as Shepherd's Pie and Irish Stew. Remember to save room for their Tall Boston Cream Pie.

Entertainment: Live music every night with a traditional seisiun on Sundays and a beginner's seisiun on Wednesdays.

What's In A Name: The pub is named for it's owner, Joseph O'Shea.

Squealing Pig

335 Commercial St., Provincetown
508.487.5804

open daily 11am 'til 1am

Rustic charm, well worn benches, tables and stools; the simple uncluttered decor gives the impression "The Pig" has always been part of the P-Town scene. Genial and approachable; the unpretentious staff aims to make you feel at home. Everyone is welcome here, there's no "type;" you'll rub-elbows with crusty old sailors, preppy college kids, Irish tourists, wall-streeters, fantastic drag queens, etc. Exceptional servings, a warm environment, a neighborly staff and a unique clientele. We really dig this "Pig!"

Food: Lunch and dinner. Pub-grub, salads, sandwiches, burgers, etc. The burgers are colossal, juicy and delicious. The Fish & Chip's are also first rate.

Entertainment: Pub Quiz Wednesdays. Friday and Saturday nights feature the biggest and best live bands from The Cape, Boston and New York. A splendid juke box. Huge screen TV for all the events.

What's In A Name: Named after a pub in Ireland of the same name.

PubCorner.com

An Cu Liath

11 Kelley Square, Worcester
508.754.6100

**open Fri & Sat 2pm 'til 2am,
Sun - Thu 2pm 'til 1am**

An Cu Liath is the proper centerpiece to rejuvenated Kelley Square. This unpretentious little pub is a major player in the improvement and revitalization of its neighborhood. A true taste of Éire, this pub mimics the craic and warmth of the rural public houses of Ireland. An Cu Liath is a tranquil oasis after a busy day at work. During the day and early evening it's the perfect spot to meet friends and linger over a pint and a good chat. Later it gets quite lively and becomes more of a party spot. The service is cheery and reliable. They set the proper mood by making the correct clientele feel at home; troublemakers and riff-raff are not welcome. They pour a pint expertly, and have a fine selection of single malt whiskies and small-batch bourbons. An Cu Liath is a must visit, but come prepared for a remarkable pub experience, absolutely satisfying even to the most demanding Irish pub connoisseur.

Food: No kitchen, but call in from the pub and have it delivered to the bar. Menus are available from Tony's Pizza, Kelley Square Pizza and Wings Over Worcester.

Entertainment: On Mondays they host the An Cu Liath City Run, a fun-run through Worcester's Canal District with complimentary post run food. Wednesday is Dart League. Thursday is Team Trivia (wicked fun). Friday and Saturday features live music. They also have dartboards, electronic/video games, large screen TV, 1000 Watt sound system, KENO, TVG live horseracing.

What's In A Name: An Cu Liath is Irish for greyhound. The owners are fans of the breed and respect them greatly, so much so that they named their pub for after them.

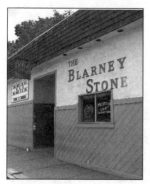

Blarney Stone

77-79 Maywood Street, Worcester
no phone

open daily 2pm 'til 2am

Simply one of the best "good time" college pubs ever. If you're looking for loud music, inexpensive drinks and attractive college students, the Blarney Stone is your pub. A friendly regular crowd hangs here during the week, a great place to relax, shoot some pool and play darts. On weekends a festive and frisky crowd takes over and uninhibited joviality reigns. A personable and professional staff guides the mirth and never let's things get too out of control. The Blarney Stone has been in the business of "FUN" for many a year and because of their expertise we know they'll be making-many-merry well into the future.

Food: No Kitchen, but all the free popcorn you can eat. If you're looking for something more substantial phone in to you're favorite sandwich or pizza shop in and have it delivered to the bar.

Entertainment: Darts, Ring-Toss, Pool, Golden-Tee.

What's In A Name: Named in honor of the famous stone at Blarney Castle in County Cork. Kiss the stone and you'll be blessed with the gift of gab.

Breen's

18 Cambridge Street, Worcester
508.799.2808

open daily 10:30am 'til 2am

Breen's is the hidden gem of Worcester and maybe our favorite new edition to this book. We're from Boston but, we gotta say, "Cheers" should've been set in Worcester; right here at Breen's. It's got it all; a horde of loyal regulars who all seem to know each other and truly caring, hands-on ownership. About the decor, we'll just mention the leprechaun. When you're there...and you honestly must visit this place...look up at the ceiling. There you'll find, smiling back at you, a huge painted leprechaun...holding a Schlitz.

Food: Breen's offers up fantastic food at incredible value. The menu is tavern fare and the owner is up at the crack of dawn shopping for fresh food each day. The burgers are tremendously popular (try the Breen's Burger). There are different specials each day and you wouldn't believe how good they are. A mound of melt-in-your-mouth Steak Tips for $7.50? Just another day at Breen's.

Entertainment: TVs for watching the games and the lively banter with your pub-mates.

What's In A Name: The pub's name comes from its original owner, Danny Breen, who opened the place after prohibition was repealed.

Christopher's

7 Pleasant Avenue, Leominster
978.534.8250

open daily 8am 'til 2am

Christopher's is a tidy, laid-back Irish-American bar filled with friendly people. The wonderful downtown location leads to a great mix of customers. An outstanding conversation bar, you'll mix easily with good-natured locals and professionals from the surrounding businesses. New faces are always welcome and are soon converted to regulars. A caring staff makes all feel at home. A congenial pour and pricing that will not bust the budget helps you relax after a busy day. Christopher's has been in business for many a year for the simple reason that they run a tavern correctly. We know this agreeable little pub will be around well into the future.

Food: Light appetizers and snacks.

Entertainment: Darts, in-house dart league. Karaoke and a couple of video games.

What's In A Name: When opening this pub 25 years ago, the owners named it after their newly born son and grandson Christopher. Christopher is now involved in the operation of the pub.

Conlin's Corner

110 Cleghorn Street, Fitchburg
978.345.2279

open daily 11am 'til Midnight

Conlin's Corner is a clean, neat and extremely well cared for pub. This old-school American-Irish bar is absolutely amazing. It's like a bar museum, walk through the doors of Conlin's and into 1962. The nostalgic décor is authentic, and adds to the unique "Average-Guy" atmosphere. The prices are from the past too; so affordable your cheapest friend will be inspired to buy a round. Entertaining regulars and good-natured bartenders make you feel like one of the gang. This is first and foremost a darts bar. The walls are lined with private dart stalls that help you focus on your game without the worry of being punctured by a stray dart. If you're a true pub fan Conlin's Corner is a must visit.

Food: Pub grub; appetizers, chicken wings, burgers, etc.

Entertainment: Pool and Darts. Men's dart league on Tuesdays; women's on Wednesdays.

What's In A Name: The owner's family name is Conlin and the pub is on a corner. Enough said.

Creegan's

165 Green Street, Worcester
no phone

open daily noon 'til 2am

Creegan's has a traditional Irish pub feel and décor with plenty of seating scattered throughout the pub. A large bar leaves lots of room for bending elbows. A relaxing outdoor patio for the warmer months. Competitive pool matches in the back room. A great dance floor, which seems to attract the loveliest young ladies in Worcester. Creegan's is a quiet pub during the day, the perfect place to meet friends for a pint and conversation. Later at night Creegan's evolves into a wicked-fun and sometimes a bit wild nightclub, always safe but definitely pushing the limits of merrymaking. A great variety of beers, 10 on draught and 50 in bottles. All the best Irish Whiskeys. Top of the line "top-shelfers" used in perfectly mixed cocktails. Easy on the wallet prices. The staff is top-notch and the bartending superb. Creegan's does all the pub-stuff correctly, the right atmosphere for each event. We totally agree with their motto, "Greegan's is the place where the good times flow!"

Food: No kitchen.

Entertainment: Live music on Saturday night, local, national and international acts (no cover charge). All sporting events shown on huge plasma screens in HDTV. Pool. Dart Tournament on Sunday, Dart Leagues on Tuesday and Wednesday. Thursday Night Poker Night hosted by The Eastern Poker Tour. DJs or live music on Thursday and Friday.

What's In A Name: The pub was named in honor of the owner's grandmother, whose maiden name was Creegan.

Doherty's

377 Park Avenue, Worcester
No phone

Hours vary

Doherty's is a neat, handsome and very compact pub. The perfect size for a local hang, a great place to rub and bend elbows with friends and neighbors. Fair pricing and a caring staff.

Food: No kitchen.

Entertainment: Plasma TV shows the games. Decent sound system.

What's In A Name: Legend has it that one of the past owners was named Doherty.

Donnelly's

43 Summer Street, Lunenburg
978.345.7757

open Tue - Sat 11:30am 'til 2am,
Sun & Mon 4pm 'til 2am

Donnelly's is a classic Irish-American tavern. Samuel Cole opened the original tavern here in 1734, thus making this the location of the oldest continually operated restaurant in the nation. They have a good-sized fully stocked bar and plenty of cozy booths. The employees are friendly and kind, the bar-staff is young and attractive, and the waitresses treat their customers as part of the family. There's a good mix of native Irish and American born patrons of all ages who mesh well in the neighborly atmosphere. There is a large function room available for private parties and events.

Food: A large variety of appetizers, soups, salads, pasta dishes, pizzas, Fish & Chips, super sandwiches and "Big Mouth" burgers. Legendary favorites include the Prime Rib Au Jus, Charbroiled Outback BBQ Ribs and Tender-Sweet Fresh Scallops. Kid's menu and take-away available.

Entertainment: Plenty of TVs for the games, Internet Juke Box, some video games and a pool table.

What's In A Name: In 1734 Samuel Cole opened a tavern on this spot catering to hungry stagecoach passengers travelling through. His tavern offered a welcome rest stop with excellent food and service. In 1983 the Donnelly family established their pub and restaurant continuing the long tradition of quality at this location.

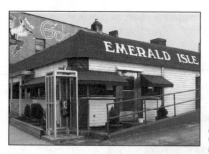

Emerald Isle

49 Milbury Street, Worcester
508.792.3830

open Mon - Fri 11am 'til 2am,
Sun 11am 'til 1am

Well worn but not tattered this pub has absorbed years of comradely joy which you sense as soon as you walk through the door. A caring staff watches over warmhearted locals. Sports, politics and basic pub philosophy dominate the conversation. Questioning anything? Emerald Isle is the answer. Why? Why not?

Food: Popular spot for lunch and dinner. The food is simple and delicious with oversized servings at undersized prices. Sandwiches, salads, burgers. All the Irish comfort entrees, the Shepherd's Pie and Corned Beef & cabbage are fantastic.

Entertainment: Pub Quiz on the last Thursday of each month. They cover all the games on TV. A great juke box. Keno. The main entertainment is the cast of interesting characters who patronize this pub and the banter they toss back and forth.

What's In A Name: Ireland is known as the Emerald Isle.

Fiddler's Green

19 Temple Street, Worcester
508.795.0400

open Fri & Sat noon 'til 2am,
Sun noon 'til 11am, Mon 5pm 'til 11pm,
Tue - Thu 11:30am 'til Midnight

Located upstairs at the Ancient Order of Hibernians, Fiddler's Green simply offers the most authentic Irish atmosphere in the city. Traditional Irish pub décor; lots of café seating, a wonderful bar and walls covered in Irish artifacts. Skillful bartending and an accomplished staff will treat you to an extraordinary pub experience. Step into Fiddlers Green and step into Ireland.

Food: Everything is homemade with the freshest ingredients. Your favorite Irish and American dishes. The desserts are made from scratch and are totally awesome.

Entertainment: A little bit of everything, always offering something new and interesting. Live music on Friday nights featuring Folk, Rock and Soft Rock. Traditional Irish Session on the 2nd and 4th Sundays of each month. Competitive darts, really fun Trivia, Texas Hold 'Em, Chess.

What's In A Name: Years ago they had a "Name The Pub" contest with members of the AOH. Fiddler's Green, the title of an old Irish song, won the contest. Fiddler's Green is where honest and upstanding Irish fishermen go when they die. Here their souls can relax, enjoy their pipe, a pint and good music, a fisherman heaven.

Worcester's Celtic Cross

In September, 1976, a magnificent, 15 foot high Celtic Cross was unveiled on the Worcester Common, commemorating the 150th anniversary of the first permanent Irish settlement in the city.

Funky Murphy's

305 Shrewsbury Street, Worcester
508.753.2995

open daily 11am 'til 2am

Funky Murphy's is a chic, contemporary version of a traditional Irish pub, an appropriate reflection of a more fashionable Ireland. The front room features the bar and the atmosphere is fun and uninhibited, a wonderful place to meet and make friends. During warmer weather large windows are opened to refreshing summer breezes, and Paris style café dining is available on the patio. The more private back room is filled with booths and tables and is perfect for social dining. The staff is hip, friendly and professional. The patrons are cordial and approachable, a good mix of post college professionals. Funky Murphy's is a great example of a modern Irish pub that has not lost that time-honored Irish ambience.

Food: Hearty, healthy and fresh, the menu features American and Irish fare with a twist. Delicious pub-grub that takes risks and succeeds.

Entertainment: Three big plasmas and a huge projection TV cover all the sporting events. Known as one of the best places in Worcester for live music. Great bands performing traditional Irish, folk, classic and current rock.

What's In A Name: An Irish surname with a cool intro conveys the character of this pub.

Galway Bay

186 Stafford Street, Worcester
508.753.8909

open daily 11am 'til 2am

Galway Bay is a lovely family-owned and operated pub. A handsome and well cared for establishment; it's always extremely clean and comfortable. A large horseshoe bar offers plenty of seating; all well within view of the attentive bartenders. An honest and friendly staff attracts a super affable clientele from the neighborhood and beyond. Very reasonable prices and they brag of pouring the best Guinness in the area. Visit the Galway Bay Pub for the perfect ambience, good food, friendly people and fair prices; it's the pub where you'll feel like part of the family.

Food: A full menu of tasty pub food and much more. Salads, sandwiches, burgers, etc. People come from miles around for Galway Bay's delicious steak tips.

Entertainment: Pool, KENO, a great Jukebox. 3 big plasma TVs cover all the games. Live music on Friday and Saturday nights, featuring best local rock and classic-rock acts. Darts are a big deal here and many a dart champion has called The Galway Bay their home pub.

What's In A Name: The pub's owner is from Galway, on Ireland's west coast. Galway is Ireland's 3rd largest, and fastest growing, city.

Hooligan's

29 Blossom Street, Fitchburg
no phone

open daily 2pm 'til 2am

Hooligan's is one of the area's best live music venues. The staff is young, attractive and fun but still professional. The ownership is hands-on and always available. The crowd is mostly a mix of "twenty somethings" from one of the colleges in the area. The $3 pitchers may advertise how cheap Hooligan's is, but this pub never lacks in quality of beverage or lack of service. A true party spot, it can get a bit wild here, but there is never any trouble. A very cute bartender informed us, "I've been here for a while and I've never seen a fight."

Food: Limited bar style menu with nachos, hot dogs, grilled chicken sandwich. Every Wednesday is Spaghetti Supper Night, free with valid student or military ID.

Entertainment: The area's best bands entertain Wednesday thru Saturday with traditional Irish taking the stage at least once each month. TV for the games, pool table, 3 dart boards with private dart stalls, KENO and a jukebox.

What's In A Name: At first guess you may think the name Hooligan's refers to their uninhibited patrons, but that's not entirely true. When the owner's grandmother was young and would go out on the town for a beverage or two with friends, her boyfriend (the owner's grandfather) would joke; "She's out carousing with hooligans." Her grandfather's sense of humor has lived on making the pub's owner a professional "Hooligan's" proprietor.

Irish Times

244 Main Street, Worcester   508.797.9599

open daily 11am 'til 2am

The Irish Times is popular with all age groups. A wonderful menu and 4 floors of fun with a variety of dining and entertainment experiences. A most proficient staff serves a large variety of ales, lagers and stouts, great cocktails and all the top shelf necessities. In Worcester The Irish Times is where it all happens, the most popular place in town.

Food: Lunch and dinner. Delicious appetizers, soups, salads, sandwiches. The gourmet fire grilled burgers come highly recommended. Irish fare includes Bangers & Mash, Shepherd's Pie and Ale Battered Fish & Chips.

Entertainment: Live music Thursday thru Sunday featuring the best cover bands. 1st floor pub offers a uniquely shaped bar that seats 20 and five cozy booths; three plasma TVs for every sporting event and a stage for live music. 2nd floor is a billiard room with a regulation table and a lounge area. The 3rd and 4th floor have been transformed into the city's hottest nightclub   "REHAB" featuring DJs and live music.

What's In A Name: The pub is named after the newspaper The Irish Times.

J.P. O'Hanlon's

9 Main Street, Ayer
978-772-9282

open Mon - Sat 11:30am 'til 11pm,
Sun Noon 'til 8pm

J.P. O'Hanlon's is a sharp looking pub located in downtown Ayer. They have over 25 draughts on tap, a wide variety of fine Irish Whiskeys, and a great wine selection.

Food: J.P. O'Hanlon's menu is a mix of standard pub fare with traditional selections. Some favorites are the Shepherd's Pie, Guinness Pie, Bangers & Mash and Fish & Chips. If you're there at lunch we suggest the Rueben O'Hanlon sandwich.

Entertainment: Irish seisiún on Sundays 5 'til 8pm. There are TVs and a dart board.

What's In A Name: The original owner's family name is Hanlon. In ancient Ireland the Hanlons were brave chieftians.

Leitrim Pub

265 Park Avenue, Worcester
508.752.0502

open daily 11am 'til 2am

Named "Best College Bar" by Worcester magazine in 2007; Leitrim is a big, raucous party spot that's the favored destination of Worcester's college crowd. They're known for fast, efficient service no matter how big the crowds may be. There are often drink specials and across the board Leitrim is always wallet-friendly. A committed ownership strives to ensure that Leitrim always delivers to its patrons. Their motto is "When the day is done and the night has come, forget the club; head to Leitrim Pub!"

Food: No kitchen.

Entertainment: Thursday is College Night. DJs Wednesday through Saturday. Plenty of TVs, pool, darts, video games.

What's In A Name: Leitrim is one of the counties of the Republic of Ireland and is part of the province of Connacht. Its name derives from the Irish Liath Druim, meaning "grey ridge."

Mahoney's

413 Park Avenue, Worcester
508.755.8876

open daily 1pm 'til 1am

Runner-up for "Best College Bar" in Worcester Magazine's 2007 Best Of Worcester awards; Mahoney's is a small, smart looking pub with a casual attitude. The decor alludes to the owner's love of horses as the walls are adorned with racing prints and old racetrack posters. Quiet during the day, this place really gets hopping at night; especially on weekends. Mahoney's is a great destination on those nights when you want to let your hair down.

Food: No kitchen.

Entertainment: Plasma TVs and video trivia.

What's In A Name: The pub is named for its owner, John Mahoney.

McFadden's

50 Front Street, Worcester
508.755.4339

open daily 11am 'til 2am

This is a new edition to the McFadden's group of pubs, which are among the nation's premier bars and restaurants. A huge room, with distinct areas, McFadden's caters to whatever you're looking for; from food to sports to a raucous night out with your friends. They combine a cozy Irish pub atmosphere with a vibrant nightlife scene.

Food: Food served 'til 11pm. The menu is upscale in taste, but not in price and features "Great American Pub Food" along with some dishes from back home in Ireland. The Flat Iron Steak is outstanding.

Entertainment: Trivia on Wednesdays. Thursday is College night with a DJ and games with prizes. There are TVs all over the pub, including 17 huge plasmas.

What's In A Name: The McFadden's pubs are named after their original location; McFadden's on Second Avenue in New York City.

Mickey Shea's

324 Electric Avenue, Lunenburg
978.342.5825

open Sun - Wed 11am 'til 1am,
Thu - Sat 11am 'til 2am

Newly opened in 2007, Mickey Shea's is a sharp looking pub where fun is always the top priority. Comfortable layout, you'll always have a TV in view and it's easy to mingle with fellow patrons. Very popular with sports fans, especially if The Sox or Pats are playing. The college crowd has discovered Mickey's, and they flock here on weekends during the school year.

Food: The menu is a nice selection of poplar choices for hungry pubbers. The portions are good and the food is tasty and filling. The cheeseburgers are very popular.

Entertainment: Karaoke on Wednesday. They have plenty of TVs, pool, darts, a jukebox, plus Golden Tee and Buck Hunter.

What's In A Name: One of the pub's owners is named Mickey while the other recently had a daughter he named Shea.

Moynagh's Tavern

25 Exchange Street, Worcester
508.753.9686

open daily 8am 'til 2am

Worcester's oldest licensed bar, Moynagh's is dripping with history and maintains an aura of days gone by. This is as authenticly old-school as you can get, and we highly recommend putting it on your short list of "must visits." One of their early patrons was none other than Babe Ruth. In fact, the bar is made of a lane from the old upstairs bowling alley where The Babe bowled.

Food: No kitchen, but there's a window for ordering from the Ivy Cafe next door.

Entertainment: Folk Music on Saturdays. There are TVs for watching the games and darts.

What's In A Name: The pub has been owned and operated by the Moynagh family since opening in 1935.

Moynihan's

897 Main Street, Worcester
508.753.6150

open daily 11am 'til 2am

An old school pub that's wearing it's years well, Moynihan's is something of a neighborhood institution. Some of their loyal patrons have been coming here for over 20 years. The bartender will greet you with a smile and make sure you leave wearing one as well. This pub is quite popular with the Clark University crowd, attracted by Moynihan's friendly prices and straight-forward attitude.

Food: The food at Moynihan's consists of familiar pub choices such as burgers, wings and grilled entrees. The extra-lean burgers are their specialty.

Entertainment: Live entertainment including karaoke and bands Thursdays and Saturdays. There are TVs, a pool table, jukebox, video games and KENO.

What's In A Name: The pub has been in the Moynihan family since opening in 1933.

Mulligan's

121 West Main Street, Westborough
508.366.0207

open daily noon 'til 11pm

Mulligan's is a friendly, family-owned restaurant where they treat you like their neighbor, not like just another customer. They offer a range of settings, from a cozy pub area, to an intimate dining room by a fireplace, to a large elegant dining room to their summer favorite - a deck overlooking the golf course. Run by long-time Westborough residents Mike and Deb O'Regan; they look forward to serving you.

Food: Kitchen open 'til 9pm. Mulligan's serves American cuisine with some interesting choices. There's an extensive lunch menu packed with burger, sandwich and wrap options. The dinner menu includes steaks, seafood and pastas. They serve a great Guinness & Beef Pie.

Entertainment: Traditional seisiun on Thursday nights. TVs in the bar for watching the games.

What's In A Name: Owing to their location at Westborough Country Club, the owners chose the name "Mulligan's." In friendly golf, a mulligan is a second chance after you've hit a bad shot.

O'Connor's

1160 West Boylston St
Worcester
508.853.0789

open Mon - Thu 11:30am 'til 11pm,
Fri & Sat 11:30am 'til 10:30pm

O'Connor's is Worcester's premier Irish restaurant. Settle into one of the many nooks, crannies and snugs and relax. The decor is all authentic Irish memorabilia. The restaurant side of things has won many prestigious awards and the bar is a fine one too; serving a wide variety of drafts, fine wines, and single-malt scotches. 30 draft beers on tap, fine wines, Irish and Scottish single malts.

Food: The menu at O'Connor's offers American and European selections along with traditional Irish fare served in ample portions. Favorite dishes include Brendan's Legendary Potato Pizza and their "famous and enormous" Beef, Mushroom & Guinness Pie.

Entertainment: 4 TVs for catching the game. European soccer shown.

What's In A Name: Brendan and Claire O'Connor, with sons Rory and Eamon, are hosts and proprietors of the pub. We have to add that meeting folks like the O'Connors is truly one of the joys of writing these books.

The Old Timer

155 Church Street, Clinton
978.365.5980

open daily 11:30am 'til 10pm

The Old Timer, "at the sign of the shamrock," was opened by Jack McNally in 1929 and is an institution in these parts. Its not unusual to find three generations of a family sharing good times at this wonderful pub.

Food: The Old Timer's menu is a very extensive collection of traditional pub favorites. The Triple Decker sandwiches and burgers are popular with the lunch crowd. Roast Beef buffet served Wednesday and Sunday from 4pm 'til 8pm. Kids menu available.

Entertainment: Tuesdays are Trivia Nights. TVs for watching the games. Live music Wednesday and Sunday during Roast Beef Buffet.

What's In A Name: When asked about the name Irene McNally, wife of current owner Jim, rolled her eyes. She's been asked this question many times. When Jim's father John opened his pub in 1929 he named it The Old Timer. He never told anyone why and no one knows. A little mystery in life is a good thing.

Slattery's

106 Lunenburg Street, Fitchburg
978.342.8880

open Fri & Sat 11:30 'til 2am,
Sun - Thu 11:30am 'til 1am

Opened as a neighborhood tavern in 1934, Slattery's has become a cherished Fitchburg institution. They maintain that old-school ambiance in their "Front Room Tavern," with it's great horseshoe bar and cozy Irish snugs. The big back room is a bit more modern, but none of the warmth is lost. Outdoor dining is offered on their terrace. Over 30 beers on tap.

Food: There's over 100 items on Slattery's menu running the gamut from salads, soups, sandwiches and wraps to Mexican, healthy "spa" options, reduced carbs meals, vegetarian, pastas, steaks, seafood and more. Sunday afternoon "Wine Dinners." Corned Beef & Cabbage Dinner served every Thursday.

Entertainment: Seven TVs and a huge HDTV. Pool table. Live music on Saint Patrick's Day.

What's In A Name: The pub has been in the Slattery family since opening in 1934.

Tammany Hall

43 Pleasant Street, Worcester
508.791.6550

open daily noon 'til 2am

Tammany Hall is the oldest continuously operated music club in Worcester. Their rich history includes a period when Tammany Hall was a speak-easy during Prohibition. They've played host to bands such as The Cars and J. Geils; on the way up, before they made it big. It is now the premier live music venue in Central Massachusetts featuring talented local, regional and national acts.

Food: No kitchen.

Entertainment: Live music every night. Blues, Classic Rock, Folk, Oldies, Rock. Two billiards tables, Golden Tee Golf, Trivia Whiz, 4 large screen TVs.

What's In A Name: Tammany Hall was the Democratic Party political machine that played a major role in controlling New York City politics from the 1790s to the 1960s. In its heyday it's electoral base laid predominantly with New York's burgeoning Irish immigrant constituency.

Tara Pub

62 Green Street, Worcester
508.757.6098

open Mon - Sat 8am 'til 2am,
Sun 11am 'til 2am

The Tara is a fun little corner pub that serves a diverse collection of regulars. It's unpretentious in its appearance and jovial in its attitude. Great value on the drinks here and a superb barstaff.

Food: No kitchen.

Entertainment: DJ on Fridays. TVs for watching the games including 2 big plasmas. Pool and darts. There's also a jukebox, video game, and pinball machine.

What's In A Name: The Hill of Tara ("Hill of the King"), located near the River Boyne, is a long, low limestone ridge that runs between Navan and Dunshaughlin in County Meath, Leinster, Ireland. It contains a number of ancient monuments, and, according to tradition, was the seat of Árd Rí na hÉireann, or the High King of Ireland.

Wexford House

503 Shrewsbury Street, Worcester
508.757.8982

open Sun - Thu 11:30am 'til midnight,
Fri & Sat 11:30am 'til 1am

Wexford House is a comfortable and very popular restaurant/pub. During the day it's bustling with retired locals and people from the nearby hospital drawn by its outstanding food at very reasonable prices. At night you'll find sports fans gathering around the bar to watch the games. Wexford House is very popular late-night with workers from the many restaurants along Shrewsbury Street.

Food: Wexford House serves an eclectic menu of American tavern fare and Mediterranean entrees. Allen Erickson, former chef at the El Morocco, runs the kitchen here. Specials are offered daily.

Entertainment: TVs for watching the games.

What's In A Name: Wexford is a maritime county in the south-east of Ireland, in the province of Leinster.

SOUTHERN NEW HAMPSHIRE

Biddy Mulligan's

1 Washington Street, Dover
603.749.1100

open daily 4pm 'til 1am

This superb pub is located in a renovated 19th century mill building on the banks of the Cocheco River just below Washington Street. Relax on their beautiful outdoor deck overhanging the river. Mingle with friends and make new ones. Strike up an interesting conversation with an attractive UNH grad-student. Their selection of bottled beers and drafts keeps all tastes satisfied. Always enjoyable and entertaining; Biddy Mulligan's is a world-class pub.

Food: Irish and American cuisine. Hearty serving sizes cooked with care. Sensational Appetizers, Soups (Flavorful Beef Stew), Sandwiches, Burgers, Steaks, and your favorite Irish classics; Bangers and Mash, Fish and Chips, Shepherd's Pie.

Entertainment: This is the spot for live music. Pub Trivia on Mondays. Rock & Roll with Tim & Friends on Tuesdays. Wednesday is open mic night (witness the best amateurs around). Thursday delightful Irish Music. The best DJs and live bands play Friday, Saturday. Pool league on Sundays. Billiards, TVs for the games.

What's In A Name: The pub's name comes from the traditional Irish song about a famous Dublin street vendor, "Biddy Mulligan, the Pride of Coombe."

Kelley's Row

421 Central Avenue, Dover
603.750.7081

open Mon - Sat 11:30am 'til 1am, Sun noon 'til 1am

Two floors of fun, downstairs is the main bar, a comfortable dining space and great outdoor deck overlooking the water (there's live entertainment on the deck during the summer). Upstairs there's smoke-free dining and the live music venue. This is no ordinary pub, they insist you leave your anxieties at home and focus on a good time. Kelley's Row doesn't have the same-old bar vibe, you'll definitely feel a warmhearted energy flowing through the staff and their customers. You'll meet easy going pubbers of all ages and be catered to by a staff that learns your name and drink. Experience fantastic pub fare, a stimulating atmosphere and exciting entertainment. Since I still had to work the next morning, my only criticism of Kelley's Row is...it's way too much fun.

Food: The menu offers a wide variety of award winning chowders and stews, fresh salads, appetizers, burgers, sandwiches, seafood, steak and barbequed entrees.

Entertainment: Seisiun on Tuesday. Karaoke on Thursday. Bands Friday and Saturday. Second Saturday each month is Comedy Night. Pool, video games, jukebox.

What's In A Name: One of the pub's owners is Brian Kelley.

Killarney's

9 Northeastern Blvd., Nashua
603.888.1551

open daily 11am 'til 1am

A picturesque pub with a cozy country cottage feel. Kilarney's resembles a pub you would find on a small country road in Ireland, not hidden away in a hotel in New Hampshire. Super neighborly, everyone knows your name. The genuinely welcoming staff puts on a fine exhibition of bartending each night. Who knew?... Irish pub nirvana found in a Holiday Inn.

Food: Lunch and dinner. Great appetizers, pub grub and terrific nightly specials.

Entertainment: Karaoke on Tuesday night. Live solo musicians Thursday through Saturday. 2 pool tables, video games including Golden Tee Golf.

What's In A Name: Killarney is a town on the Ring Of Kerry in southwest Ireland. The name is derived from the Gaelic Cill Áirne and means "Church of the Sloes." The sloe is the fruit of the blackthorn tree which is found in abundance in the area.

Knot Irish Pub

60 Main Street, Durham
603.868.2959

open Mon - Fri 5pm 'til 1am,
Sat noon 'til 1am, Sun 9am 'til 1am

The Knot is a terrific little Irish Pub located across from the UNH campus. It's got a sharp yet casual style, with polished wooden floors and richly painted walls. They serve fresh and hearty fare at prices any college student would love. Drink specials are offered each night. There's a lot of craic packed into this small space. This is "knot" a pub to miss.

Food: The Knot's menu includes pub favorites such as burgers, wings, etc. along with expertly prepared Irish classics including Shepherd's Pie and Bangers & Mash. In fact, the chef buys his bangers from the Olde Irish Butcher Shoppe in Stoughton, MA and they're truly fantastic. Breakfast, including full Irish Breakfast, is served on Sundays 'til 1pm.

Entertainment: Live bands Tuesday, Wednesday and Friday. There's a TV for watching the games, darts, a jukebox and a checkerboard.

What's In A Name: Celtic knots are a variety of knots and stylized representations of knots used for decoration, adopted by the ancient Celts.

McGarvey's

1097 Elm Street, Manchester
603.627.2721

open Mon - Fri 3pm 'til 1am,
Sat & Sun noon 'til 1am

As much a great American saloon as an Irish pub; they know the bar business here and they do it right. McGarvey's is a friendly neighborhood pub, a great place for meeting friends after work or before an event at the Verizon Wireless Arena. A banner waitstaff and bartenders who unapologetically serve mean cocktails. Fun local regulars. For a good pour and a good time - visit McGarvey's.

Food: All your pub favorites, burgers, sandwiches, etc. Great Chicken Wings.

Entertainment: Karaoke Friday, Saturday and Monday. 2 pool tables, darts and TVs for all the games.

What's In A Name: The owner is a sailor. On a visit to Baltimore to inspect a boat he was considering buying he visited a place called McGarvey's. He loved the pub so much he named his pub "McGarvey's" in honor of it.

Molly Malone's

177 State Street, Portsmouth
603.433.7233

open Mon - Sat 11:30am 'til 1am
Sun 10:30am 'til 1am

Located in an old, elegant, red-brick building; Molly Malone's offers a first floor dining area and a lively second floor pub with a magnificent granite bar.

Food: Molly Malone's has developed quite an exemplary reputation for its food. Everything; from the seafood chowders to the hand-cut steaks and Sunday brunch, is top notch. Molly's was named "Best Brunch In Portsmouth" by the national publication "Where Locals Eat."

Entertainment: Trivia on Sundays. Karaoke on Wednesdays. Live Irish music Thursday and Saturday.

What's In A Name: The pub is named after the famous fish monger from Dublin. "Cockles and Mussels! Alive, alive, oh!"

Murphy's Tap Room

494 Elm Street, Manchester
603.644.3535

open daily 11:30am 'til 1am

Newly opened in 2007, Murphy's Tap room is a traditional Irish neighborhood pub infused with American modernity and diversity. 24 beers on tap and over 20 bottled selections. Happy Hour is 4 'til 6pm daily and there are drink specials each night. Ask about their "Mug Club." You get your own shiny 20 ounce mug that'll be waiting at the bar for you, plus discounts and perks.

Food: Murphy's serves a high-quality pub style menu with some great Irish choices. They boast of the best Shepherd's pie in Manchester. The burgers are extremely popular here and there's a nice selection of burger options. Save room for dessert, and we'll recommend the Black & Tan Brownie Sundae to finish things off.

Entertainment: Irish music Monday through Wednesday. Rock Thursday through Saturday. 4 huge flat-screen TVs carrying all the games. Pool, darts, foosball and Golden Tee Golf.

What's In A Name: The pub is named for its owner, Keith Murphy.

Murphy's Tin Palace

2 Ballard Street, Durham
no phone

open Mon 5pm 'til 1am,
Tue - Sat 11am 'til 1am, closed Sun

Recently renovated and re-opened after a fire, Murphy's Tin Palace is a totally happy little pub. Located next to UNH, you'll be partying with a young and lively crowd. Murphy's is a popular spot all year round but the fun really flourishes during the school year. Sidewalk cafe seating is offered during the warmer months. This outdoor patio is a great place to linger over a pint and a good chat, and watch the world go by. Tasty food, great entertainment, attractive college co-eds and capital cheer, Murphy's Tin Palace never disappoints.

Food: A full lunch and dinner menu offers burgers, sandwiches, salads, wraps, pizza, and daily specials. They have such yummy appetizers that many customers order a few different apps as their meal. Great Steak Tips. Munch away!

Entertainment: Open Mic Mondays. Trivia on Tuesdays. Live bands Thursday through Saturday and a DJ downstairs on Thursdays. Plenty of big plasmas, darts, 2 pool tables, jukebox and Golden Tee Golf.

What's In A Name: The pub was previously owned by Mike Murphy, who took over a bar named The Tin Palace.

O.K. Parker's

89 Hanover Street, Manchester
603.645.1106

open daily noon 'til 1am

Billed as "A Good Irish Tavern," OK Parker's is a busy and fun pub located in downtown Manchester. This place could quickly become one of your favorites.

Food: OK Parker's serves up standard pub grub. The Buffalo Wings are outstanding.

Entertainment: Pool table, Golden Tee Golf. Pinball, Video Trivia, TVs.

What's In A Name: The pub is named for Ted Parker; owner of several pubs over the past 30 years. Ted's an "OK guy."

O'Leary's Grille

816 Lafayette Road, Hampton
603.926.4343

open daily noon 'til 1am

O'Leary's is a sprawling sports bar. In fact, a mecca for sports enthusiasts. This large pub is laid out well, with distinct areas for you and your mates to congregate and mingle. Year round they do a good business with loyal locals, and in summertime new faces from the beach are added to the mix. They plan on adding a huge wrap-around outdoor deck to bring that summer fun up a notch.

Food: O'Leary's serves up American tavern fare along with fresh seafood. The pizzas are very popular and they boast of the best seafood on the New Hampshire coast.

Entertainment: Live bands on Saturdays. There are plenty of TVs including 5 big plasmas. 3 pool tables, darts, video games and a cool jukebox.

What's In A Name: The pub takes the family name of the father and son owners.

Peddler's Daughter

48 Main Street, Nashua
603.821.7535

open daily 11am 'til 1am

The Nashua Peddler's Daughter is both a lounge-music venue and a restaurant; and is laid out in a rustic design. They're known for their great, warm atmosphere, and serve up some of the best pub grub available.

Food: The Peddler's Daughter serves up high-quality pub fare. Some favorites are the Guinness Braised Beef Stew and the Pub-Style Meatloaf. Great Flat Bread Pizzas.

Entertainment: Pub Quiz on Tuesday. Live bands Wednesday, Thursday and Saturday. DJs on Friday. Lots of TVs.

What's In A Name: Haverhill, site of the original Peddler's Daughter, has had its share of successful business and professional people, but it is doubtful that anyone was more widely known than Maggie Cline. Maggie was a vaudeville star. Her father, Patrick, was a peddler.

Shaskeen

909 Elm Street, Manchester
603.625.0246

open Mon - Fri 11:30am 'til 1am,
Sat & Sun 10am 'til 1am

The Shaskeen is a magnificent pub in the heart of downtown Manchester. It is the creation of traditional Irish musicians Tommy and Louise McCarthy along with Matt Molloy, flute player with the Chieftains. It's a grand venue for music and they attract some of the best traditional musicians you'll ever see. The atmosphere is warm, friendly, and authentically Irish to make you feel like you are back in the auld sod.

Food: The Shaskeen offers wonderful pub favorites and traditional Irish dishes. The food is superb; fresh ingredients and expertly prepared. Don't tell mom how good their Chicken Pot Pie is, it'll break her heart. Daily "Pizza Of The Day." Brunch and Irish Breakfast is served on weekends.

Entertainment: Live traditional Irish music 7 nights a week. Set Dancing classes on Wednesday nights (beginners welcome). One TV.

What's In A Name: The pub is named after the famous traditional Irish tune The Shaskeen Reel. Shaskeen also means marshy land otherwise known as the bog.

Wild Rover

21 Kosciuszko Street, Manchester
603.669.7722

open Mon - Fri 11am 'til 1am,
Sat & Sun Noon 'til 1am

Opened in 1990, The Wild Rover offers classic Irish pub appeal. The 100 year old oak floors and brick walls set the tone. They have one of the largest draft and microbrew selections you'll find; and boast an authentic Belgian Draft Tower. Great place to stop in before or after an event at the Verizon Wireless Center. A shuttle to the arena is available on event nights.

Food: The wonderful menu at The Wild Rover offers up familiar pub fare and "not-so-pub" specials. A few good recommendations are the Nacho-Crusted Chicken Sandwich, Lamb & irish Sausage Stew, and Bison Burger. Specials daily.

Entertainment: Irish sing-along on Wednesday and Thursday. Golden Tee Golf and a jukebox. TVs for watching the games, including Setanta Pub Channel and Gaelic Games. WiFi internet access.

What's In A Name: The pub is named after the popular Irish song "The Wild Rover."

We hope you enjoyed our guide.
Please look for our other titles
at Amazon.com and fine bookstores
and gift shops.

There's much more for pub
lovers at our website; so we invite
you to visit.

Sláinte!

PubCorner.com